L.I.F.E.

Learning Information
For Everyday

L.I.F.E.

Learning Information For Everyday

Social Skills

Beth Carey

L.I.F.E. Learning Information For Everyday

ISBN 978-0-9967548-2-8 (paperback)
ISBN 978-0-9967548-3-5 (eBook)

Library of Congress Control Number: 2017901952

Published by:
Trail Ahead Publishing
Woodstock, Georgia

Table of Contents with Checklist of Topics

Feel free to check off topics as questions are answered and subject matter is mastered.

Introduction

Here it is ... *L.I.F.E. (Learning Information For Everyday)* *Book 2 — Social Skills.* It's the Grand Canyon of topics from which teens can benefit! I feel obligated to include everything, as this is the subject nearest and dearest to my heart. The use of expected behaviors, etiquette, courtesy, whatever you want to call it, is a daily expectation like brushing your teeth (for me anyway). It's something I believe all humans, not just teens, should be practicing routinely which is why I am sharing the topic with you!

Before using this book, know that I will be addressing topics and situations many teenagers might feel they will never encounter (e.g., proper table settings, valets, bathroom attendants, golf course personnel, black tie affairs, etc.). Some teens cannot envision oral and written communication beyond what they use currently. The thought of needing to learn proper introductions, business letter formats, and gift giving practices doesn't resonate with them. **However, one thing I have learned in my lifetime is that adults frequently end up in situations they never anticipated when they were young**. Therefore, the goal of this book is to prepare individuals for both present *and* potential scenarios. I, myself, never imagined attending a black tie affair, dining in a place where I was given multiple forks to use, or having to introduce executives to my children — but life required all this and more. **Since no one can predict the future, it's important that adolescents (and the adults helping to prepare**

them for the future) keep an open mind and not let economic, regional, cultural, or social environments of today preclude learning something that might be needed down the road. *To get the most from this book, I am asking that readers keep the scouting motto of "be prepared" in the forefront of their minds.*

I also want to inform you that I like to write in a relaxed and conversational manner (you will notice this rather quickly and I hope it puts you at ease). I often use parentheses for my own personal voice or as a way to add an additional comment that doesn't fit into the normal dialogue. Since I believe the best way to really embrace and influence teenagers is with some humor, don't be surprised if you find these sidebars sarcastic in nature. (After all, good etiquette doesn't mean you're devoid of humor!)

For the entirety of this book, the word "teen" or "teenager" will be used to represent all youth, ages 10 to 20 years old.

Realize that I do not claim to be an all-knowing human being with every answer when it comes to teens. However, after earning a master's degree in Vocational Leadership, teaching high school for 30 years (in the public and private sector involving classroom and administrative experience), having sponsored DECA (an organization for marketing students), and having raised two children of my own (Ben and Leah), I come to you with relevant insight. *This book is a collection of observations and information to ideally help adults as they prepare teens for adulthood.* (Although I have come to understand many teens are reading this book series on their own. Kudos to you!)

Whether you are a parent, grandparent, aunt/uncle, mentor, teacher, homeschooler, or a young person yourself, please understand this book has the most positive outcomes when open dialogues occur *between* adults and teens. Since developing rapport isn't always easy, the questions within are designed to help get the process started. Once the treasure chest is unlocked, barriers will crumble and all sorts of questions, answers, and conversations will result (I promise).

Adults, I ask you to keep conversations with teens free of judgments. Teens will shut down in a heartbeat if they think you are being hypercritical or even a little critical of them (or worse yet — being hypocritical). Let teenagers share their ideas, feelings, and thoughts on social skills (or any other topic for that matter). Then help *guide* them to learn the skills and information within these pages to ensure they avoid negative consequences and embarrassment for not knowing appropriate behaviors and expectations of our culture. Make it a game. Slip questions in at dinner or during a car ride. Text a daily question or ask a question at the end of a class period each day. Make asking the questions as natural as possible and teens will start to look forward to the engagement.

Teens, if you are the reader, I ask you to connect with a reliable and trustworthy adult for clarity and a deeper understanding of the information within this book. Be cognizant that asking an adult for assistance is not a crime or as "uncool" as you may think. It serves as a networking opportunity and will make you more confident, independent, and ready for the world. You can challenge yourself in a game-like fashion by answering the questions and then checking the answers to see how you did. (I hope you get them all right too!)

The format of this book is similar to Book 1, but since I can't assume everyone has read *L.I.F.E. — Challenging Your Teen's Basic Knowledge*, I will give a brief overview. (If you have utilized Book 1 — feel free to skip this part if you don't need or want the review.) Let's get started.

The *L.I.F.E.* series is divided by topic area. Each chapter starts with a list of *questions, tasks, discussion points, and/or vocabulary* to challenge knowledge and skill base. A brief introduction leads into the *truth and consequence* segment which provides information to illustrate the need for this topic. Then the *answer key* follows with further explanations and details.

The topics can be tackled in any order. Do all the questions in one sitting; tackle one subject at a time, or shuffle chapter questions. Consider having a "question of the day" or "topic of the week." Note that there are no multiple choice questions (guessing through process of elimination is not what we're striving for here) and there are no lessons on sex, drugs, coping, or emotional matters. (There are abundant resources on those subjects if needed.)

Keep in mind that although some answers could vary with ethnic, regional, economic, or lifestyle differences, I try to stick to common ground in answering the questions and expounding on the subject. I believe what is presented is the *minimum* information needed to prevent teenagers from becoming overwhelmed and frustrated as they prepare for their next phase of life. Therefore, I encourage readers to go into more depth and do research when applicable.

In contrast to Book 1, where *stories* told revolved around negative consequences, this book shares both positive and negative outcomes related to social actions taken by individuals. I hope you enjoy the true stories (with many names changed to protect the innocent— LOL) as they provide humor and illustrate social skills applied (or not applied) in the real world by both teens and adults.

Each chapter will end with a *Let It Go* suggestion. These are things that "just aren't worth the fight" in today's world. Icons, throughout the book, identify the different components I just described and will make utilizing *L.I.F.E.* easy.

Here is what each icon stands for:

QUESTIONS (topic questions to check for knowledge, skill, and understanding)

ANSWER KEY (answers to the questions to clarify and assist)

TRUTH & CONSEQUENCES (rationale to explain why this topic is important)

NOTE (sideline pieces of information you may enjoy or find helpful)

TO DO (activities to check for know-how instead of oral responses)

STORY (true stories to illustrate need for topic at hand and for fun)

STEPS (list of steps to make learning a concept easier to follow)

DISCUSSION (questions that will involve dialogue of give and take responses)

LET IT GO (suggestions for things that aren't worth the fight with this generation — it demonstrates an understanding that the teen generation and perhaps the world in general, has changed)

One last thing — you may notice in Book 2 that there is a subtle change in my target audience. In the first book, I addressed adults who I hoped would engage teens by asking the questions provided. However, because I found that many teens were reading this series on their own, I have tried to write to include those readers (rather than writing to adults about them). *The goal is to talk to you, the reader, without assuming your age group.* See if you can tell the difference. And remember that even if a teen uses the book as a self-exam, he or she still needs someone older and wiser to serve as an advisor for further explanation and discussion. Two-way learning and communication will be most effective!

Remember that there is no blame or shame for not knowing any of these social skill topics, so "no pressure" (regardless if you are an adult or teen). Be proud of the journey you are undertaking. Understand that these questions relate to important, sometimes controversial, and culturally diverse subjects. (Heck, sometimes there are differences in social guidelines just going to different parts of the same town!) Be flexible, tolerant, and have some laughs along the way. I wish all adults and teens good luck as you journey through *L.I.F.E.*!

⑦ General Etiquette

1. What does "gratuity" mean?

2. What does "going Dutch" mean?

3. When receiving the following services, how much should you tip in the U.S.? (Hint: can be a percentage or specific dollar amount)
   - ☐ barber/hair stylist
   - ☐ barista
   - ☐ bartender
   - ☐ bathroom attendant
   - ☐ bellman/porter/storing valet
   - ☐ coat/hat check attendant
   - ☐ food delivery person
   - ☐ golf personnel
   - ☐ hotel/motel maid
   - ☐ manicurist
   - ☐ parking valet
   - ☐ server at buffet restaurant
   - ☐ server at full-service restaurant
   - ☐ supermarket bagger/courtesy clerk
   - ☐ take-out service personnel
   - ☐ taxi driver
   - ☐ rideshare driver

4. How do you calculate gratuity (tip) on a bill?

5. When interacting with sales clerks, servers, home maintenance workers, receptionists, etc., what are some things to keep in mind related to the treatment of these individuals?

6. Who is responsible for holding a door open, the male or female?

7. If given a name tag or badge to wear, is it placed on the left or right side of your chest?

8. When using an elevator, what do you do to demonstrate proper etiquette?

9. When on escalators or moving sidewalks, what should you remember to do?

10. List 5 etiquette guidelines that should be followed when using public transportation (e.g., bus or subway).

11. When approaching a closed door in a home, what should you do before entering the room?

12. When approaching a closed door in a work setting, what should you do before entering?

13. If you approach a room (in the home or office) with an open door and hear people talking, what should you do?

14. When borrowing items from others, what 3 rules apply?

15. When you see "RSVP" on an invitation, what does it mean?

16. List 3 behaviors a good host/hostess should exhibit when someone visits their home.

17. What is a host (or hostess) gift?

18. What type of items are appropriate to give a host or hostess?

19. When choosing a gift for someone, what ensures it will be "special"?

20. What do you do if you receive a gift you do not like or will not use?

21. What does "regift" mean?

22. Is it OK to "regift" an item?

23. Is it within good etiquette guidelines to ask for someone's Wi-Fi password?

⑨ General Etiquette

How often do we witness young people (or not so young people) needing improvement in basic etiquette or manners? You know … not introducing a new member to the group, not putting a cell phone down at the dining table, not responding to an invitation with "RSVP" on it, or not tipping properly. What about wearing inappropriate attire to a function? And have you ever had to fight your way off an elevator because those entering didn't wait until you exited? (I see you nodding your head.)

Based on research and discussions with others, I propose the following list of top etiquette faux pas (in no certain order) — see what you think:

1. lack of "please," "excuse me," "thank-you," and "you're welcome"
2. clothing choices inappropriate for occasion or age
3. improper dining behavior
4. inappropriate hand gestures and/or vulgar language
5. being loud and rowdy in a public place
6. lack of precautions related to bodily functions
7. personal space and property violations
8. arguing and/or talking back to elders
9. inappropriate use of cell phones
10. poor writing and oral communication skills (virtually and in person)

How did I do? Do you agree that our society may be struggling with many of these points? And just what is etiquette anyway?

Well, for this discussion I am defining etiquette as "a system of rules or norms that have been established to guide social and professional behavior." (Is that what you had in mind?) Additionally, manners are considered to be similar and will be defined as "the prevailing customs and behaviors of a society of people." Let's throw in a splash of politeness and courtesy, "consideration and respect in attitudes and behaviors towards others," as part of this conversation and there you have it. So, let's move to the truth and consequences of this subject.

Some of the Generation Y adults (often called the Millennial Generation), born between 1980 and 2000, have been accused of thinking "all this etiquette stuff is hogwash." Generation Z (those born after 2000),[1] frequently follow with the same mind-set. So, is it only the "uptight, over 40-years-old generation" that cares about how a person goes about behaving and interacting with others?

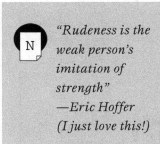

"Rudeness is the weak person's imitation of strength"
—Eric Hoffer
(I just love this!)

Author Alex J. Packer, PH.D., conducted a survey in 2014 that resulted in:

1. 73% of the teachers and 75% of the parents stating that students today are less polite than they were as students. (Isn't it interesting how each generation is convinced that society is less polite now than when they grew up?)
2. 71% of the teachers saying that today's adults are less polite.[2]

---

1 http://www.talentedheads.com/2013/04/09/generation-confused/
2 Alex J. Packer PhD, "How Rude! Teacher Survey: Today's Kids: Polite or Not?" http://www.alexjpacker.com/blog/2014/10/25/7mikpf6be0g6tyywy066o37qv710hw

Additionally, Stageoflife.com surveyed teens resulting in:

1. 70% of teenagers reporting they feel society, as a whole, displays more bad manners than good manners.
2. 91% of teens saying that civility, manners, and etiquette are either "very important" or "important" in their lives.[3]

Influencers of poor etiquette include parents, siblings, friends, teachers, and all the media.

Good etiquette exceptions:
1. *physical or mental limitations*
2. *emergencies when time is of the essence*
3. *on rare occasions when all parties in your inner circle agree to "completely chill" in the privacy of a home*

So, why aren't more people practicing etiquette and manners routinely? Has it truly been a slow and steady decline, or do we all just look to blame someone else for the changing times?

Here is the truth of the matter: *if a person's actions, words, or behaviors are interpreted as rude by anyone, then there is a problem and one must take stock of that and re-evaluate.* It is not a sign of weakness to be "kind" or "proper." And if the newest generation (nicknamed the "I-Generation") is too me focused, too stressed, or too inattentive to courtesies (all accusations being tossed around), then apparently everyone must share the blame. Once people stop pointing fingers, general etiquette changes will happen and that is the vision in this chapter.

I have found with teenagers that when they understand the reasoning behind the "rules," they buy into the practices more

---

3 http://www.stageoflife.com/StageHighSchool/OtherResources/Statistics_on_High_School_Students_and_Teenagers.aspx

quickly. (Hence I encourage sharing the "why" along with the "rule.") Here are a few very practical reasons for some of the expectations in the U.S. today. See if knowing the "why" behind the "rule" makes you feel better about these examples and then pass on the knowledge.

Rule	Rationale
No elbows on the table	• elbows take up additional room • there is the possibility of hitting your neighbor • dirt is transferred to the table as one doesn't wash elbows before meals • in history, it was seen as a sign of hunger and poverty to lean toward food
Moderate use of perfume/cologne	• people have allergies and sensitivities to fragrances • others may not enjoy the scent
Removing hats indoors	• hats originally were worn for weather protection which is not necessary indoors • removal ensures that the person behind you will not have blocked vision • in history after a battle, helmets and hats were removed as a sign of peace and respect which is still the case
Sending a thank-you note	• ensures that the giver knows the gift was received and appreciated

Did having the rationale help ease the pain of having to follow a "rule" for you? (I hope so.)

Although etiquette guidelines can be dictated by regional or cultural practices, using a *middle of the road approach* will make sure behavior isn't rude, distasteful, or unacceptable and goes a long way in reducing harsh consequences (one of my main goals in writing this book). Demonstrating etiquette can have a huge payoff when interacting with those who award college admission/scholarships, as well as those who provide reference letters, make job offers, give promotions or raises (not to mention scoring big points with

Know that charm and even the best of etiquette practices is no guarantee that you will always get what you want, but it sure can't hurt.

the parents of one's girlfriend/boyfriend or the people living next door). And since the best way to react to rudeness or bad behavior is to ignore it, I sure don't want to see young people set-up to become invisible as they venture out into the real world. When one meets societal expectations of common courtesy, they are more likely to ensure *others* feel comfortable, confident, and self-assured. (How awesome is that?) Plus, knowing the "rules" reduces stress and takes the guesswork out of behavioral choices.

The first chapter starts with *General Etiquette* because I want future generations to know:

1. What it means to be civilized.
2. That one should treat others better than they want to be treated.
3. Sometimes a person just needs to conform — like it or not.
4. Manners say something about a person's character and desire to be "a cut above" (a phrase my Dad loved to use meaning a person does more than an average job — this person goes above and beyond expectations).
5. A person's etiquette and use of manners is a reflection on them, their associates, and *does matter!*

Here's What A Teen Needs To Know ...

I.   What does "gratuity" mean?

⑨   An additional gift of money, over the cost of a
     service rendered (i.e., tip)

📕   *Ashley just started working at the Olive Garden Italian Restaurant
     and was making $2.13 an hour, plus tips. She greeted her guests, got
them drinks, suggested item choices, and took the orders. She then helped
prep the salads, served the food, refilled drinks, and got the little girl an
extra dipping sauce. Ashley cleared the family's dishes and remained
cheerful the whole time while serving additional tables. Everyone ate
the meal without complaint, but left no tip. Ashley was confused as she
served the family well.*

Really???? I ask you, have you ever been a waiter or waitress?
Have you ever had a job that required being on your feet for eight
hours and responding to demands from someone? And if so, did you
get paid more than $2.13 an hour?? (I bet you did!!)

I always told my students to remember that the waiter/waitress
didn't overcook the steak; the chef did. Don't take it out on them
and leave no tip. If service is poor, patrons should ask to speak to a
manager. A short changed waitress will complain to her co-workers
as she rubs her sore feet, assume the guest forgot, and might question
her job selection, but will not equate the lack of tip to unsatisfactory
service. Leaving no tip is not fair especially if one is just trying to
save money. When partaking in an activity that traditionally is
gratuity driven, one must plan for it in the budget.

Although Ashley's guests were not teens, teens do have a reputation for being small tippers. Why is that? I like to believe that teens

often don't know proper tipping etiquette. (If they did, they would do the right thing.) And although the tipping system in the U.S. may seem unreasonable when compared to other parts of the world (where tipping isn't required), if you live or visit the U.S., you should know the drill. Just because you may not like the system, that isn't a valid argument for not tipping. Teenagers must learn the guidelines and practice calculating a tip in their heads (although most will use a tipping app 😄).

"TIPS" stands for "To Insure Prompt (or Proper) Service." Just a fun fact!

2. **What does 'going Dutch' mean?**

     Each participant pays their own way

"Going Dutch" (also known as *Dutch date* or *Dutch treat*) has meant paying separately for decades. There are numerous stories describing where the term originated, but no one is sure. Anyway, "going Dutch" is not to be confused with "splitting the bill" where each person pays half. When you "go Dutch," each person pays for only the portion that he/she consumed or used.

3. **When receiving the following services, how much should you tip in the U.S.?** (Hint: It can be a percentage or specific dollar amount)

     Presented are the average *suggested* tip percentages or amounts with brief elaborations (Keep in mind these are suggested guidelines, but no one typically complains if you tip too much.)

Service	Suggested Tip
barber/hair stylist (person who cuts and styles hair)	<ul><li>10–20% is the average.</li><li>Varies depending on personal opinion and geographic area.</li></ul>
barista (person trained in making and serving coffee drinks or the like)	<ul><li>The "tip jar" is optional, but typically patrons drop change or $1 into the jar.</li><li>It's your choice, but consider tipping in places where you are a regular.</li></ul>
bartender (person who makes and serves drinks in a restaurant or bar)	<ul><li>$1 per drink ($.50 for non-alcoholic beverages) or 15%–20% of the total bill (tip more in venues you frequent often and in large city areas).</li><li>Consider tipping after each drink to help ensure exceptional service throughout the visit.</li></ul>
bathroom attendant (person providing assistance to patrons usually in high-end establishments)	<ul><li>Bathroom attendants are to be tipped if they provide some type of service and aren't just "standing watch."</li><li>Tip $.50–$3 (some attendants provide only a hand towel, hence $.50 — others may provide grooming accessories, help remove a stain from clothing, repair a hem, or offer a shoe shine — tip accordingly).</li></ul>
bellman/porter/ storing valet (person who stores, moves, or retrieves baggage in a hotel, rail station, airport, etc.)	<ul><li>Tip $1–$2 per bag</li><li>Pay more if bags are extra heavy or numerous.</li><li>Tip more in large metropolitan areas and in more expensive venues.</li><li>It's a good idea to base the tip on the value of what is being stored (it is nice to assume people are trustworthy, but a better tip may help encourage honesty and care).</li></ul>
coat/hat check attendant (person who stores items at event facilities and restaurants)	<ul><li>$1 per coat or hat minimum (Yes, these do still exist!) and more if the item is expensive.</li><li>Consider tipping when you drop off and when retrieving an item.</li></ul>

Service	Suggested Tip
food delivery person (person delivering pizza, Chinese, groceries, etc.)	▪ This really depends on the distance the driver has to go from the restaurant to your house, condition of food when delivered, if service takes place during peak hours, size of order, how hard it is to get to your door (e.g., apartment on 3rd floor with no elevator; it's raining), and the cost of total food bill. ▪ 10%–20% of the grand total is typical. ▪ If there is a "delivery fee" assessed automatically by the company, check to ensure this fee goes to the delivery person. If the establishment keeps the fee for "their trouble," then tip the person at your door.
golf personnel (person who assists golfers with cart, gear, food, shoes, etc.)	▪ $3–$5 per bag to person helping at bag drop area or $5 a cart. ▪ $2–$5 for club cleaning and assistance to your car after the round. ▪ $3–$5 locker room attendant tip for shoe cleaning and other assistance. ▪ 15%–20% tip to beverage cart personnel while on the course or in the restaurant/ bar. (When playing at a private club, tips are typically not allowed as membership fees include payment for club personnel services.)
hotel/motel maid (person who cleans and maintains supplies in your room)	▪ $2–$5 per night, paid as a lump sum at checkout, but daily is best as different staff members work different days. (It would not be fair if you had the same housekeeper for three straight days and the fourth day she was off and didn't get any of the tip.)
manicurist (person who cares for hands and nails)	▪ 15% of total bill.

Service	Suggested Tip
parking valet (person who parks a car at a restaurant, hotel, or building)	• There are many options and opinions for this one, but definitely pay when your car is retrieved. You may also pay when the car is taken to be parked and probably a good idea especially if the car is an expensive one. • Tipping $2 a car is standard with up to $5 for the nicer venues and for valuable vehicles.
server at buffet restaurant (person who clears plates, refills drinks, checks on you, etc.)	• $1 per person or 5% of the total bill is customary. • If you are a regular, tipping more is common.
server at full-service restaurant (person who takes your food and drink order, serves you, and is available throughout a meal if you need something)	• 15% for adequate service and 20% (or more) for exceptional service, high-end restaurants, or restaurants in major cities (calculated before sales tax although most people tip on grand total because it is easier). • Restaurants often add gratuity to the bill for a table of six or more people, so check. If this automatic tip isn't warranted, managers will make adjustments. • Calculate the tip before any discounts or coupons are applied. • If service is really poor, let the manager know and leave 10% or less. Placing two pennies, side by side, on top of the check is an indication that service was unacceptable and explains why the server received less than expected. • If you occupy a table for an extra long time, tip more (especially in a crowded restaurant). • Tip more if you are a frequent patron to ensure the best service. • Since breakfast meals result in a lower overall total, tipping a higher percentage is commonplace.

Service	Suggested Tip
supermarket bagger/ courtesy clerk (person who bags groceries, assists patrons to their car, maintains parking lot, etc.)	▪ Tip amount depends on the number of bags. $1 - $5 (unless there is a sign that says "no tipping please"). ▪ If you are escorted to your car with bags, given help with loading, and provided cart management, take that into consideration.
take-out service personnel (person who takes order and packs food orders not to be eaten in-house)	▪ No tip is needed, but always appreciated. Sometimes there is a jar marked "tips" by the cash register to place money. ▪ Tip more if you are a frequent patron to ensure the best service.
taxi driver (professional driver who transports passengers to their chosen destinations)	▪ 10%–15% of total fare with a $2–$5 minimum (20% is typical in larger cities).
rideshare driver (driver contracted through an app to transport passengers to their chosen destinations)	▪ Tipping practices vary with provider.

Mary Helen was in New Orleans and had taken a taxi to an office building for her business appointment. She arrived at her destination very quickly, thanked the driver as she paid the fare on the meter, and gave him a 20% tip. Thirty minutes later she realized her cell phone was still in the taxi. Just as she started to comb through her memory to recall the name of the taxi service, the receptionist called into her meeting room and asked if she lost her phone. The taxi driver had come back to the office to return the forgotten phone. Mary Helen mentioned to the room that it must have been her 20% tip that caused the driver to repay the kindness and go out of his way to return her phone. The business associates agreed.

Tipping is hard for many people to do properly, particularly those on a tight budget. I suggest two things to teenagers since gratuity is not compulsory in the U.S.:

1. Think about the person who has provided the service. If the service provider made you feel like a priority, it will be easier to give a proper tip.
2. Remember to take into account the tip cost when planning an outing.

4. How do you calculate gratuity (tip) on a bill?

🔑 Take the total amount of the bill and multiple by the percentage of tip you want to give then add that amount to the previous total for a grand total-if giving a straight dollar amount, just add it to the bill total

I like to remind teens that if doing math in their head is not a strong suit, tip apps or the regular calculator available on a cell phone can make this process easy and accurate. Additionally, there are printed hard copy "tip charts" available that are the size of a credit card for easy wallet storage. Some restaurants have "tip charts" at the bottom of the bill and others provide a "pay-at-the-table" kiosk or tablet and the screen provides tip options. All this variety makes accurate tipping almost effortless.

 If using a coupon or any form of discount, calculate the tip on the total amount before the reduction.

5. When interacting with sales clerks, servers, home maintenance workers, receptionists, etc., what are some things to keep in mind related to the treatment of these individuals?

 Answers will vary

 This would be a good time for teens and adults to discussion appropriate treatment of siblings and classmates, physical and cyber bullying/taunting, and the devastating effects of each.

Wow! I just opened up a huge can of worms, didn't I? Make sure you allow enough time for this discussion because the etiquette, manners, courtesy, and politeness with which a person treats others says so much about their character. Regardless of age, gender, occupation, or income level, one must remember that we are all equals and everyone deserves to be treated with dignity and kindness. Keeping in mind that individuals in careers such as these are often the gateway (or gatekeeper) that determines whether you have a smooth and positive experience or not.

6. Who is responsible for holding a door open, the male or female?

 Whoever gets to the door first

In today's world, leaving the stereotypical bias of men always hold doors for women behind is definitely the way to go. I tell teens to think in terms of courtesy for a person, not a gender. Applying kindness in other similar circumstances (e.g., help pick up items dropped by someone, assist with storing luggage in overhead bins on planes, lend a hand to carry things, give an elderly person your seat on the bus, aid a parent by taking the shopping cart back to the corral so they can stay with the kids at the car, etc.) is along the same principle as the door holding and should start at an early age.

Erica (a Down syndrome student) was trying to make her way to class on Tuesday morning with an arm full of books, her lunch box, and a tote bag. Two guys went running by while playfully pushing, shoving, and berating each other without regard for bystanders.

Boom! Down went all of Erica's stuff.

Kurt, who witnessed the event from a nearby locker, grabbed his marketing book and slammed his locker. "Hey!" he yelled towards the boys who were halfway down the hall oblivious to their actions.

I entered the hallway when I heard the yell and saw Erica standing frozen with tears welling in her eyes. Before I could say anything, Kurt walked over and started picking up her things. He handed her the lunchbox and tote bag first. He then stacked her books on top of his, smiled at Erica, and said, "Mrs. Carey, I'm going to take these books to her room. I'll be back in a minute."

I nodded as I beamed with pride. The bell rang as I watched my sweet student walk the now much less upset Erica around the bend.

7. If given a name tag or badge to wear, is it placed on the left or right side of your chest?

Right

It seems like this shouldn't matter, but the rationale is two-fold. First, because humans typically greet each other with a hand shake, you will want the tag/badge to show. Think about it. As the right hand reaches out to grasp another hand, the right shoulder naturally turns slightly toward the person you are greeting. This moves the tag/badge forward and allows your name to be seen more clearly as the left side actually turns away from whomever you are speaking too. (Remember from Book 1, learning becomes easier when more of the five senses are applied? So, help a guy out and let him see your name as you say it — increasing the chances that he will remember you.) Secondly, companies put their logo (graphic symbol or words specific to company) on the left side of shirts (at least the ones who know better). You don't want to cover those logos up, so stick to the right in all occasions.

8. When using an elevator, what do you do to demonstrate proper etiquette?

Here is a list of proper etiquette, but give credit for all reasonable answers:
- Allow everyone to exit before trying to enter
- If first on, hold the door open (physically or with door open button on the control panel)
- Offer to push the floor button for everyone if you are closest to the control panel
- Contain personal belongings and make room for others
- Assist and allow elderly and physically impaired people more room
- Discontinue conversations once doors close (including phone conversations)
- Face forward

- Announce "my floor" to alert others of your need to exit
- Move aside (or step out of elevator) to allow others room to exit

I could write pages outlining the numerous scenarios and preferred actions that relate to elevator behavior, but let's skip all that and get to the bottom line. The goal is to patiently help people get onto the elevator, push needed floor buttons, and make opportunities to exit.

 Many elevator etiquette behaviors can also be applied to travel on trains, subways, buses, etc.

Once on the elevator, allow each person to have as much personal space as possible. Be aware that if it is crowded, you may have to "body-up," while minimizing direct physical contact (hopefully everyone showered that day-LOL).

When exiting a crowded elevator, the people in front should get off first (common sense). A person in the back, will need to signal movement to those blocking the doors by saying "excuse me" or "my floor" (unless you just plan to take a joy ride to the upper floors). Those in the front can simply step aside or step out of the elevator to allow others space to exit. I like to use my hand/arm to hold the door open if no one has pressed the "Door Open" button on the control panel. This is courteous and guarantees I will be able to get back in before the doors close (self-preservation idea, for sure). Men should stand back and allow women, children, elderly, and those impaired to exit first (like a rescue mission off a sinking boat), but that may only be possible with small crowds.

9. When on escalators or moving sidewalks, what should you remember to do?

 Stand on the right side so others can pass on the left

Sometimes people choose to walk instead of standing still or they may be in a hurry, so be aware and don't stand in the middle. (Signs are often posted to serve as a reminder.) While passing, simply say "excuse me" and move by quickly.

Remember to hold the rail for safety and be patient. Don't stop at the top of an escalator or in the middle of a sidewalk to talk, tie a shoe, get something from your bag, or to re-group. This is inconsiderate and can cause a collision.

10. List 5 etiquette guidelines that should be followed when using public transportation (e.g., bus, train, subway).

 Answers may include:
- Step away from doorways so others can enter and exit easily
- Have fare money ready
- Give seats to the elderly, mothers, women, and the disabled
- Don't place backpacks, purses, and briefcases on seats
- Share the pole with others
- Keep voice low
- Use earphones for music
- Avoid cell phone conversations
- Talk to strangers with caution

- Avoid using or eating anything that has an odor (popcorn, fish, perfume, nail polish, etc.)
- Avoid sharing germs (e.g., cough or sneeze into your bent elbow)
- When feasible, women, elderly, and disabled individuals should be allowed to enter first and get off second so men can assist if needed

11. When approaching a closed door in a home, what should you do before entering the room?

🔑 Knock and wait for an answer to welcome you inside

Family was visiting from out of town and everyone went to bed. Chris had gone to the bedroom he was assigned to for sleeping and forgot his phone charger in the family room, so he ran back to grab it. The door was closed, but he walked right in. Mechelle squealed and quickly turned her back to Chris as she had just pulled her shirt off.

"Sorry!" Chris exclaimed as he backed out of the room closing the door again. "Didn't know anyone was sleeping in here. I just need my charger."

"That was awkward, Chris. Glad I turned around so quickly. Try knocking next time."

"My bad. Again, I'm sorry."

"It's OK. Just give me a minute and I'll give you the charger as soon as I get my robe on."

This is a good time to review the fact that a closed door in a home usually means "off limits." If a person needs to enter a room (e.g., the bathroom), knocking is the best way to check to see if anyone is already utilizing the room. If 10 seconds go by and no one replies, then entering would be appropriate (assuming this is a room one would have permission to use).

I like teens to know it is never OK to "knock and walk" — you must wait for a reply. Additionally, if you knock and someone responds, wait for an invitation to enter to avoid any embarrassing moments. Respecting privacy is key to a peaceful home existence.

12. When approaching a closed door in a work setting, what should you do before entering?

 Depends

This question may seem premature for teenagers, as many have not started working yet, but the knowledge will be needed someday. And although "depends" may not seem like a good reply, there is no clear-cut right or wrong answer. If an associate is known for keeping his door open and it is closed on a particular day, then one should turn around and walk away. Send a message via email or text and tell this person you would like to speak to them. Unless it is a true emergency, knocking is a bad idea in this case.

On the other hand, if a co-worker always keeps his door closed, knocking may be the norm. One way to handle things is to watch how other co-workers handle the closed door. Teenagers need to understand that they should never enter until being invited to do so.

13. If you approach a room (in the home or office) with an open door and hear people talking, what should you do?

 Make the occupants aware of your proximity

If people are talking, in or out of a room, here are the options: knock on the open door itself, tap on the door frame, clear your throat, or simply announce a "Hi!" or "Hey" to alert those conversing. To avoid eavesdropping or startling anyone, it may be best to turn away and come back later.

14. **When borrowing items from others, what 3 rules apply?**

> Take good care of whatever is borrowed, return it in a timely manner; replace the item if something happens to it

The shower felt so good after a long day of work. I climbed in and let the water wash away all the stress and tension. I washed my hair and while the conditioner worked magic, I reached for my razor, but it was not on the shelf. I looked behind me to the other shelf and nothing. I spun around and still nothing.

"Leah! Leah!! Leah!!!"

"Yeah Mom. What's wrong?" she yelled back as she ran toward the bathroom door thinking I had hurt myself.

"Where is my razor?" I snapped.

"Ahhh. Probably in my shower where it does not belong."

"You got that right. Now go get it!"

"Sorry Mom. I just was in a hurry and forgot."

More important than the fact that people say individuals should not share razors, Leah should have asked before borrowing my razor and should have returned it as soon as she was done using it. Remembering to return a borrowed item in a timely manner shows courtesy and appreciation to the lender. In my experience, teens can be forgetful when it comes to returning things. (What has your experience been?) Teenagers need to practice returning items promptly, so the tendency doesn't continue into adulthood. The item should be in better shape than when borrowed (if possible) and if the borrowed item is held for an extended period, throwing in a small token of appreciation like a gift card, pan of cookies, or note of gratitude is a nice touch. I suggest letting the lender know upfront how long you intend to keep the item and make sure that timeline is acceptable to them.

A friend of the family (Gerald) called me and asked if he and two friends could borrow our cabin for the weekend. There was a disc golf tournament in the town and the start time in the morning made driving from his house prohibitive. I checked the calendar to make sure we had no plans and promptly told him, "Sure!" We reviewed some instructions for the house and I sent him the keys.

The weekend following his stay, my husband and I arrived at the cabin to find on the table a disc with the tournament logo on it, $40 cash, and a thank-you note expressing that the money was to cover the utilities as well as to show appreciation. I immediately got on the telephone and called Gerald to thank him for the thoughtfulness.

15. When you see "RSVP" on an invitation, what does it mean?

 Please respond

RSVP is an abbreviation for a French phrase (répondez, s'il vous plaît) and means "please respond." When listed on an invitation, the inviter wants to know if you are or are not coming to the event (usually by a specified date). Responding as soon as you know if you can attend ensures one does not forget to inform the host. This allows the host to plan for an accurate number of expected guests and certainly would help reduce some stress.

If an invitation states "RSVP, regrets only" (or "Regrets only"), then you only need to respond if you *cannot* attend. This reduces correspondence, which is nice, but it does not lessen the need for a decision.

16. **List 3 behaviors a good host/hostess should exhibit when someone visits their home.**

Answers will vary, but could include:

- Prepare in advance for guest (clean, get supplies in, etc.)
- Greet guest at the door
- Offer to take guest's coat/jacket
- Offer guest a seat
- Offer guest drink and/or food
- Allow guest to go first (i.e., when eating, playing a game, being served, etc.)
- Ask guest what activity they prefer to do while you are together
- Show guest around (where bathroom is, what areas are off limits, etc.)
- Provide fresh linens and adequate blankets if guest is spending the night
- Tell guest to "make themselves at home"
- Walk guest to door when they leave
- Thank guest for coming

Being a good host is important, but I want to also review the etiquette that constitutes *being a good guest*. Little gestures like helping to clean off the table after dinner, stripping bed sheets after an overnight stay, or putting the board game back in the box, leave such a favorable impression. Of course, words like "please," "thank you," "yes sir" (to adults), etc. are to be used often and contributing something (food, flowers, small gift) never hurts. Showing you are an "easy guest" to have around increases the chances of being invited back!

Another life lesson for teens that fits well under this topic is the practice of *not* asking something of a parent or adult, related to a friend or colleague, *in front of* that friend or colleague. Asking for a favor with all parties present (e.g., "Mom, can Bobby sleep over tonight?" or "Ms. Bosslady, is it OK for Sue to come to lunch with us?") really puts the adult on the spot to answer in the affirmative and that is not fair. These conversations should be done in private so there is an opportunity for open dialogue. This approach results in more mutually positive outcomes and is applicable to many situations in adulthood.

17. **What is a host (or hostess) gift?**

    A token of appreciation given to the person who invited you to an event

18. **What type of items are appropriate to give a host or hostess?**

    Answers will vary, but could include:
    - Flowers
    - Wine or liquor (age dependent, of course)

- **Specialty foods/beverages** (jams, nuts, fruit, chocolate, coffee, cheeses, etc.)
- Plant
- Gift basket of lotions and soaps
- Picture frame
- Candle
- Book, magazine, music

Bill was on his way to Rosie's apartment for a "Welcome Home" party for her brother, Johnny, who was in the Navy. Bill decided it would be nice to bring Rosie a hostess gift for having this party for his best friend, so he stopped at the local florist and bought a dozen red roses.

When Rosie answered the door, Bill handed her the bouquet as he hugged her gently and looked into the room to see who had already arrived. She pulled away and said abruptly, "Bill, you know I have a boyfriend! Why did you buy me red roses when all we can be is friends?"

Bill paused for a minute and then said, "Wait. I didn't mean anything romantic with the roses. I was trying to be nice and bring you a hostess gift."

Rosie could feel her face redden from the neck up as she said, "Oh. OK. It's just red roses are a sign of love and I thought … "

"Sorry Rosie. I didn't mean to upset you. There was just a sale on roses and they were pretty!" Bill responded as he entered further into the living room while Rosie sighed with relief.

Gifts don't have to be expensive or elaborate, but they should have meaning. And when it comes to flowers, research color and types as they can be appropriate for certain occasions (e.g., Peace Lily plant for funerals, yellow flowers for friendship, red roses for love, etc.). Gifts need to fit the occasion and the person receiving them. As always, follow customs of the region or culture as giving a gift may only be needed on special occasions and not every time.

19. When choosing a gift for someone, what ensures it will be "special"?

Answers will vary, but could include:
- Meaningful or useful to recipient
- An activity or experience rather than a physical item
- Applies a memory or makes a memory
- Consideration of the recipient's likes and dislikes (not necessarily your own)
- Personalizing an item
- Purchasing something other than food or beverage (especially for a dinner gathering)
- Homemade instead of purchased
- Suitable for the particular occasion
- Age appropriate

Consider the occasion, expectation, and what you can afford before choosing a gift. An acquaintance's lagniappe should be quite different than your BFF's (Best Friend Forever) gift.

Giving a gift can be as much, if not more fun, than getting a gift if done correctly. Don't you agree? So often people associate gift quality with the price tag (you know … the higher the price, the better the gift). I propose that individuals who give gifts that create experiences and memories far outweigh a store bought present. Plus, spending too much money on a gift leads to buyer's remorse and stress if the cost results in a financial strain.

Teenagers and adults can brainstorm ideas easily. Start by recalling the top 5 gifts you have received and see if that sparks ideas for gift giving to others. Consider an IOU Coupon book, a homemade card, a hike and picnic to a nearby waterfall, a photo of the recipient's favorite sports player or one of the two of you, and so on. Be creative!

Colin and Caitlyn spent the Fourth of July week with us at the cabin and ran to town for one last iced coffee. When they arrived home, they walked in with a pot of flowers colored red, white, and blue. Colin handed me the gift as he leaned over and kissed me on the cheek. Caitlyn handed me a card and said, "Thanks again, Aunt Beth!"

"Oh kids! Our pleasure. These are lovely and so festive. Thank you!" I exclaimed while setting them on the center of the table.

> *Since teenagers tend to have better technology skills than those 20+ years their senior, offering to teach and assist with computer problem solving is often appreciated, a good general etiquette practice, and could be a nice "gift" idea.*

20. What do you do if you receive a gift you do not like or will not use?

Fake it!—be enthusiastic and appreciative of the gesture and move on

Remembering to be a gracious recipient of a gift is a skill to be learned early in life. A simple "thank you," a comment on how thoughtful it was, and avoiding "you shouldn't have" is key regardless if you like the gift or not.

> *Cards that accompany a gift should be opened and read before opening the gift itself.*

21. What does "regift" mean?

 Giving a gift, previously received from someone else, to another person

22. Is it OK to "regift" an item?

 Yes and No

This is a tricky concept. After all, when a person goes to the trouble and expense of choosing something special for you, turning around and handing it off to another human being just because you don't like it certainly would seem rude. However, I can see telling an adolescent that if she truly will not use an item and does not want to be wasteful, then regifting is similar to recycling and may be the answer.

 Here are steps to follow before regifting:

→ Be very careful not to regift in the same social circle (hurt feelings can easily result if the original giver discovers what you are doing).
→ Be sure the new recipient would truly like the gift (this isn't a chance to just unload unwanted stuff).
→ Check that the gift is unused and in its original package.
→ Ensure the gift is not of a "special" nature, chosen just for you (i.e., handmade or personalized).
→ Re-wrap gift.

I like to tell teenagers to consider giving the unwanted item as a "just because gift" to a new recipient. Explaining that "I don't need two" or "this present is something I know you would enjoy" is at least more honest than acting like the gift was specifically selected with a certain person in mind, when it wasn't.

23. Is it within good etiquette guidelines to ask for someone's Wi-Fi password?

Maybe

I don't usually allow a wishy-washy answer like "maybe" to fly, but in this case, I truly think that is the best answer. Most businesses (and some private residences) have a "Guest Wi-Fi" login that they are willing to share (some require a password and some do not). If you are going to be at a private residence for an extended stay, I would inquire as there is no reason to use all your data capacity if Wi-Fi is available. Consider saying, "Do you mind if I use your Wi-Fi while I'm here? I totally understand if you don't want to share the password, but I thought I would ask."

Just remember to not be offended if someone does not want to share their password because of security reasons. Teens (or anyone for that matter) can politely say, "I understand" and move on. If an individual isn't comfortable sharing Wi-Fi, maybe the host would be willing to share his/her device so you can at least check for important messages and such. (Time should be limited on electronics anyway if you are visiting with someone.)

///////////////////////////

I would be remiss if I didn't close this topic by reiterating that since not all people practice etiquette the same way, do research, go with the flow, be aware of the customs practiced around you, and follow that lead. Also, regardless of how you personally feel about etiquette practices, it is important to understand that people are judged on their behavior, so it's best to "play the game." Change is hard, no matter your age, so playing by the rules provides more peace and a sense of comfort. Applying general etiquette practices will get the most favorable response from others in social and career situations which is the ultimate objective. That's just a life fact!

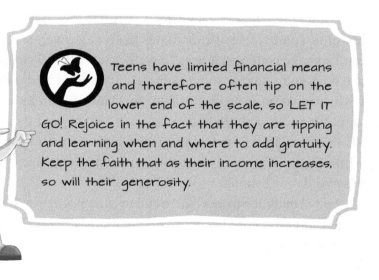

Teens have limited financial means and therefore often tip on the lower end of the scale, so LET IT GO! Rejoice in the fact that they are tipping and learning when and where to add gratuity. Keep the faith that as their income increases, so will their generosity.

(?) Personal Guidelines

1. On a scale of 1 to 10 (10 being the best), rate your eye contact and explain your response.

2. Why is good eye contact important in the United States?

3. Demonstrate a proper handshake.

4. Should a male or female initiate a handshake?

5. Define personal space.

6. In America, how many feet would be considered the average distance for "personal space"?

7. Do you talk with a distinctive accent (Southern, Boston, Midwest, New York, etc.) and is there a stereotypical bias for that accent?

8. Define body language.

Body Language - What does the following body language typically signify about how a person is feeling?

9. Arms crossed over your chest

10. Tapping your fingers
11. Resting your chin on your palm
12. Touching or rubbing your nose while giving a verbal response
13. Leaning forward towards someone
14. Staring blankly at the floor
15. Rapidly nodding your head
16. Slowly nodding your head
17. Biting your fingernails
18. Tilting your head to the right side slightly
19. Scratching your head
20. Crossing your legs if you are female
21. Twirling or playing with your hair

22. List 3 things that contribute to having "good posture."

23. What is a "social kiss"?

24. Define dress code.

 25. What does "dress appropriately for the occasion" mean to you?

26. When invited to an evening wedding, what should a male wear?

27. When invited to an evening wedding, what should a female wear?

28. What does going to a "black tie affair" mean?

29. When should a man remove his hat?

30. When should a woman remove her hat?

 31. Describe what is meant by "good hygiene."

32. Name a minimum of 3 practices that contribute to "good hygiene."

33. List a minimum of 5 activities, related to bodily functions and grooming, that should not be done in the presence of another person.

34. If someone is wearing too much perfume or cologne, how should you handle it?

35. After using the toilet, what 3 things should be done?

⑨ Personal Guidelines

Humans use their five senses of seeing, hearing, smelling, tasting, and touching every day as a vehicle to interact with others. Consequently, impressions are made (like it or not). Impressions turn into judgments and may be formed based on a combination of personal factors or just one factor. People take less than a minute to determine if they really want a conversation to continue when meeting someone new. Did you realize that the majority of that decision is based on what is seen? Statistics claim a first impression takes as little as 10 seconds to be formed, which means a person's aura is impactful. (How scary is that?) Teenagers need to be aware of how the use of their bodies can make a flattering or unflattering impression as they strive to enter the adult phase of life with success.

And think about how powerful the sense of smell can be. When was the last time a familiar odor reminded you instantly of someone because that was "their scent"? (My grandmother had a faint smell of mothballs because she kept mothballs in her closet with her clothes. — LOL) Ever have a baking apple pie or a certain perfume immediately make a special person come to mind? Regardless of whether the recipient finds a smell pleasant or unpleasant, the effect is lasting.

TC Actions, appearance, verbiage, tone, and even hygiene will be assessed when interacting with others. The impact now, and in the future, is often based solely on the way in which a person "carries themselves" (i.e., gait, posture, swagger, head position, etc.). Unfortunately (or fortunately), the critique continues even *after* a relationship develops, so your personal image is *always* on display being judged and impacting the overall opinion someone has of you.

Granted, if a person is not interested in having personal and/or professional rapport with other individuals (hermit life does appeal to some), then and only then, can he go through life oblivious to these facts. And because our species tends to draw conclusions about ourselves and those around us rather quickly, impressions are formed on personal factors. The good news is that there are guidelines to help.

I hope teens know it takes a lot of effort and time to change someone's previously formed conclusions about you, so it's beneficial to get it right the first time. Throughout life, individuals will get different reactions, rewards, consequences, and opinions from others. It is the consequences we want to minimize, so here are some questions to check concepts related to *personal guidelines.*

Here's What A Teen Needs To Know ...

 1. On a scale of 1 to 10 (10 being the best), rate your eye contact and explain your response.

 Answers will vary-discuss the answer given

Good eye contact does not come easily to everyone. This nonverbal method of communication is a skill that involves consistency without turning into a stare down. If a teen admits to not being comfortable looking others in the eye, this skill can be acquired with practice. It is possible that a teenager will not hesitate to look friends or family

As a rule, the United Kingdom, the United States, Australia, and Western Europe believe in eye contact when conversing. Middle Eastern culture dictates less eye contact than in Western cultures and the rules are not the same for men and women. Asian and Latin American cultures have a strict hierarchy belief system and frown upon steady eye contact between subordinates and superiors. So, do your homework before traveling or entertaining foreigners.

in the eye, but will look at their shoes when addressing adults or someone new.

Although many cultures have different rules about eye contact, here in the U.S., facial expressions with long glances are typical. This includes limiting blinks, acting natural, and matching the amount of eye contact given by your counterpart — keeping in mind that people have different comfort levels when it comes to eye contact. The goal is to be engaging, not creepy.

I like to encourage teens when talking in a group, to always look at the person doing the talking and try to stay focused 100% of the time. When speaking, remember to take turns looking at each person in the crowd. With practice, becoming a pro at eye contact is easy.

Ahhh ... another school year had started. The students bustled into the room — some with happy faces, some rather sad expressions, and some neutral. Slowly frowns started turning to smiles as acquaintances recognized each other and the chatting volume got louder.

I watched as Stephanie introduced Rob to Dianna and their mingling continued. Two minutes later the late bell rang and students took a seat as I introduced myself.

Just after the bell rang ending class, Dianna (whom I had in class the previous year) came up to me and asked me if I knew Rob. I said, "No. Why?"

"Well, I think he is really cute, but he doesn't look at me when I talk to him. He looked at the ceiling, at the walls, and even up at you. I wondered if something was wrong with him?"

"Now Dianna, you know some people are shy and just struggle with eye contact ... especially if a pretty, smart girl is involved." We chuckled.

"That's true, but I must tell you that all I wanted to do while we were talking was grab his face with my hands and yell, 'Look at me when we are talking you fool!'"

2. Why is good eye contact important in the United States?

⑨ Answers will vary, but here are some possible ideas:
-   Shows self-confidence
-   Demonstrates one is paying attention and interested
-   Demonstrates significance of person talking
-   Sign of trustworthiness
-   Demonstrates professionalism
-   Illustration of good manners
-   Portrays that one cares

"When the eyes say one thing, and the tongue another, a practiced man relies on the language of the first."
—Ralph Waldo Emerson

3. Demonstrate a proper handshake.

 A proper handshake should look like this

and involve the following:
- Extend right hand toward other person
- Connect by allowing the web (area between the thumb and forefinger) to touch
- Grasp firmly and shake 2-3 times up and down
- Maintain eye contact
- Drop hand to the side of the body

4. Should a male or female initiate a handshake?

 Either

 Handshake etiquette varies from culture to culture so do your homework.

In this day and age in the U.S., gender should have no bearing on offering a hand to another person. This applies in both the business and personal sector, so shake away!

5. Define personal space.

🔑 Area surrounding an individual that they psychologically believe belongs to them and therefore should not be invaded

6. In America, how many feet would be considered the average distance for "personal space"?

🔑 Approximately 3 feet in all directions

If a person wanted to study this subject in depth, there is literature out there that will categorize space requirements depending on an intimate, friend/family, social, or public circumstance (with a range of less than 2 feet to 12 feet). However, for our discussion, being aware of someone else's 3-foot invisible bubble will keep you out of trouble in the vast majority of situations. Keep in mind that everyone is unique and may require a smaller or larger boundary to feel comfortable and your connection with that person usually makes a difference (life-long friend vs. person you just met). This is similar to how some people are huggers and some are not!

Personal space guidelines are hard to follow at times as human fascination can take over and cause poor judgments. Case in point would be when a person stares at men and women with tattoos, gauges, and

 Having tattoos, gauges, and piercings is a private choice much like style of clothing. Some people love them while others find one or more distasteful. Therefore, individuals need to think about the potential consequences (short and long-term) before any permanent alterations are made to their own body.

Under certain circumstance, it is a good idea to hide your ink or conceal/remove a piercing that isn't in an ear.

piercings (as well as someone who has a disability, an unusual hair color, is wearing revealing clothing, etc.). Ogling, even from a distance, is a form of personal space invasion. Additionally, body art is not an invitation to touch, anymore than running a finger across a painting in an art gallery is appropriate. One shouldn't be too inquisitive unless a person invites you to do so or is talking about the tattoo, piercing, or gauges first (otherwise you may offend and anger someone). Many tattoos have personal significance, so be respectful of that possibility.

Max was waiting in line to check out at the grocery store. He was in the 20 items or less lane and was next. Kennedy was behind Max staring at his gauges and sleeve tattoo. Suddenly Kennedy reached up and inserted her finger through Max's right ear gauge and said, "Wow!"

Max turned abruptly towards Kennedy and snapped, "What are you doing? Are you insane? That's my ear!"

"I'm sorry. I've never seen anything like that. Why did you do that?"

"Girl, you are crazy! None of your business!" Max said as he stepped up to pay for his items and glanced over his shoulder giving Kennedy a disgusted look.

7. Do you talk with a distinctive accent (Southern, Boston, Midwest, New York, etc.) and is there a stereotypical bias for that accent?

Answers will vary-be ready for some honesty during this discussion

Due to age and limited experiences, teens often are not aware of preconceived assumptions and prejudices when it comes to speaking with an accent. That is why a dialogue is the most beneficial way to handle this topic. In the classroom, I would have frank discussions with my students in Georgia related to southern accents. I wanted them to know that many people will assume individuals to be lacking in education and intelligence because they talk with a heavy drawl and use phrases like "fixin' to" and "y'all." I explained this was *not anymore factual* than when someone assumes all people with New York accents are confrontational (facts worth mentioning).

I would also lecture to my students that being aware of possible negative prejudices is just "smart." If trying to impress someone, plan for it and make adaptations in dialect and wording — just to be on the safe side. If I can speak like I was born and raised in the South and switch to Pittsburghese (where I was born and raised) on command — anyone can do it with some practice (currently my normal voice is somewhere in-between). Teens would argue that doing this was "fake." My response was to remind them it is a choice and with every choice there is a consequence that you must be prepared for.

8. Define body language.

⑨ Communicating without words by using gestures and movements

Our body movements are like electric billboards that can't be missed. Even the slightest adjustment to our head, appendages, or face will speak volumes about what we are thinking and feeling (and can get us in big trouble). My own children and students have revealed more by rolling their eyes at me than anything they may have said! I want teens to be aware of the message given by certain body positions in the U.S. to avoid misinterpretation.

 A smile shows interest and causes a positive and upbeat environment. Use one often!

<u>Body Language</u> - What does the following body language typically signify about how a person is feeling?

9. Arms crossed over your chest

   Cautious, defensive, angry, uninterested

10. Tapping your fingers

   🛈 Agitated, bored, anxious

11. Resting your chin on your palm

   🛈 Critical, cynical, negativity towards the receiver, tiredness

12. Touching or rubbing your nose while giving a verbal response

   🛈 Doubt, dishonesty

13. Leaning forward towards someone

   🛈 Interested, trying to comprehend or hear better

14. Staring blankly at the floor

   🛈 Disinterested, avoiding eye contact

15. Rapidly nodding your head

   🛈 Urgency to add to the conversation, very much in agreement

16. Slowly nodding your head

   🛈 Positive interest, comprehension, validation

17. Biting your fingernails

   🔑 Nervousness, habit

18. Tilting your head to the right side slightly

   🔑 Open, creative

19. Scratching your head

   🔑 Puzzled, itchy

20. Crossing your legs if you are female

   🔑 Possibly flirtatious

21. Twirling or playing with your hair

   🔑 Nervous, habit

I encourage teens to do more research about body language and what it can mean — it's fascinating! Meanwhile, I suggest everyone watch excessive gesturing or talking with his/her hands (except in the case of sign language, of course).

22. List 3 things that contribute to having "good posture."

   🔑 Accept any of the following:
   • Stomach in/engage core
   • Chest out

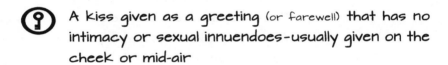

- Shoulders back
- Head up
- Feet 6-8 inches apart
- When seated, lean forward slightly from the hip

Posture sends a message related to self-confidence and portrays whether a person is approachable or not. It is the first form of body language that others notice, so teens should be aware.

23. What is a "social kiss"?

A kiss given as a greeting (or farewell) that has no intimacy or sexual innuendoes—usually given on the cheek or mid-air

This can be so awkward. Even adults have the brain debate of whether to kiss on the cheek? Kiss on the lips? Do an air kiss? Or offer only a handshake?

I suggest basing the decision on how well you know the person, what happened the last time you were together, and follow the lead of the other person. Typically, the person with higher status gets to make the decision (women being the ultimate decision maker), but this varies from culture to culture. In the U.S., social kisses occur on the cheek or lips between males and females, but on the cheek only between females. Men do not exchange kisses, but will shake hands and embrace (hug) with bold pats on the back. Social kisses are quick and usually involve a hug or handshake simultaneously.

24. Define dress code.

Set of clothing expectations (or rules) for a particular place, group, or occasion-can include accessories and shoes

25. What does "dress appropriately for the occasion" mean to you?

Answers will vary and may include:
- Referencing the dress code and choosing wardrobe accordingly
- Dressing like everyone else
- Apparel that is customary for an event
- Wearing clothes that are not offensive to others
- Dressing so you don't stand out

Clothing was originally a function of physical protection. It kept humans warm in the cold months, cool in the summer, and provided safety in many jobs (e.g., hunter, firefighter, etc.). Historically, children dressed like miniature adults and clothing choices were limited. Once television was invented, the clothing industry boomed. Clothing styles expanded for all ages and became a symbolic statement indicating social status and provided identifiable associations based on people's interests (i.e., biking shorts), memberships (i.e., Hell's Angel), and careers (i.e., nurse uniform). Additionally, clothing choice today is a statement of attitude, knowledge, economics, and self-esteem (especially for adolescents).

From my experience, teenagers dress according to how they view themselves in their current environment. They often try to make the case that their wardrobe is a way to "express their individuality." However, I have found that it is more likely a lack of knowledge related to suitable dress, the desire to belong to (or copycat) a particular social group, and a shortage of limits (financially or otherwise) by adults that drive what teens wear.

I observed, as a teacher and mother, that tweens and teens who chose age appropriate outfits and didn't show underwear, butt cracks, or cleavage, tended to get in less trouble at school. (I didn't make this up, I promise!) Additionally, these students tended to be the leaders in school. They commanded a presence through their wardrobe that was fitting of a *young adult* and benefitted from that choice. Because of this observation, I would discuss in my classroom the importance of wearing belts and socks, especially when business or more formal attire was expected. I could be quoted as saying, "Wear what you want around the house, but put some thought into public appearances."

Many homes today are "shoe free" zones. Hosts should warn you in advance of this policy, but don't act surprised or insulted if someone asks you to remove your shoes before entering.

I also liked to remind my students not to forget about keeping their shoes in good condition (free of holes, dirt, and scuffs). "You can tell a lot about a person from their shoes," I would preach (reminding them also that clothes don't have to be expensive, just in good condition). And no group discussion about appropriate dress would be complete without mentioning the fact that "overdressing" can be judged as strongly in the etiquette guru's eyes as "underdressing."

26. When invited to an evening wedding, what should a male wear?

 A suit (or sport coat with dress slacks), **belt, dress shirt, tie, socks, and dress shoes**

Regardless of denomination, a wedding held in the evening is a more formal event than a daytime affair and a guest should respect that and dress accordingly. I suggest checking out the venue to get a hint on how to dress if you aren't sure or inquire with someone in the wedding party.

Many gentleman aren't sure of the difference between a suit and sport coat/pants outfit, but it is very simple to distinguish the difference. A *suit* means the jacket

(blazer) and pants are of the *same color and fabric*. A sport coat (also called a sports coat) is more casual in nature and will be a different fabric and/or color than the pants. The most common pairing is a navy jacket with khaki pants, but there are numerous combinations. Suits typically worn to a wedding are blue, gray, or black so men add color with the tie (and shirts, depending on the current fashion craze) — just keep things within reason. Normally, no one would wear a cartoon character tie or a neon green dress shirt

Attire is important at a wedding and so is attitude and disposition. Be cheerful and remember to smile.

to a wedding, but personal taste can play a part in decision making even when dressing for a wedding.

If a wedding is being held outside or in a venue of a more casual nature (beach or back-yard, for instance), the invitation or wedding website should provide an indication. This would allow a man to scale back and leave the tie and jacket at home (maybe). Since it is better to be safe than sorry, I suggest going dressed more formally and removing garments (like a tie or jacket) after surveying how others are dressed. (I know my husband and son have stored ties in my purse on more than one occasion!)

27. **When invited to an evening wedding, what should a female wear?**

 A dress or very dressy slacks and blouse with dress shoes (hose are optional depending on the geographical region and current fashion trends)

Females have the advantage here because they have more options than males. Dresses can be long, short, or in-between. Women can substitute a blouse with pants or a skirt, if dresses "aren't their thing." Jewelry and

Unless specifically stated, jeans and shorts would never be considered wedding attire. Same goes for t-shirts, golf shirts, Hawaiian shirts (unless it is a tropical beach wedding), tennis shoes, flip-flops, or work boots. And hot weather is not an excuse to forgo the long sleeved shirt, jacket, or tie—sorry guys!

Fabric and colors are lighter in the spring/summer and darker and heavier in the fall/winter months for guys and gals. Avoid wearing the same color as the wedding party (hint: look at the colors on the invitation).

Typically, dress for a wedding is fancier than a Sunday church outfit for both male and females.

other accessories (scarves, belts, shawls, etc.) can spruce up the plainest garment and make for a classy, yet fun, wedding outfit. A wedding is a special celebration and guest's attire needs to enhance the event.

Color choices are also more abundant for the ladies. Tradition says not to wear white or off-white (as that is reserved for the bride), so just go with a color that corresponds with the season or what complements you. Know that black is no longer off limits for women to wear to a wedding. In fact, the little black dress works nicely for an evening wedding. Just do not wear anything too tight, low-cut, short, or glittery and remember to check those slits when standing and sitting.

 Consider religious affiliation of the bride and groom and do some research if you are not familiar with practices or expectations at a church ceremony.

28. What does going to a "black tie affair" mean?

Men are expected to wear a tuxedo and women to dress in evening attire ("little black dress" or evening gown)

I want teenagers to know that if you can't wear a tux or appropriate evening attire to this event, then send regrets and don't attend. Women have some flexibility, but typically this means a gown to the floor (or tea length dress). This dress does not have to be black, but typically it is black or another neutral color (avoid bold prints). Checking around to see what others are wearing or what was worn last year at the event is helpful. This is a formal, dressy affair — the goal is to look like you belong. Being remembered for what you *didn't* wear correctly is not what you want others to recall. If a person does not have a tux, one can be rented (that's what my husband does).

I was attending a black tie affair with my husband in Santiago, Chile. This was part of a business conference of top executives, from companies across the world in Tom's industry.

When we entered the ballroom, there was one gentleman who stood out in the room of 200+ penguin suits (the nickname given to tuxedos because of their white chests and black bodies). Tom and I exchanged glances and proceeded to mingle.

Throughout the night, numerous people commented directly to us about "the man in the regular suit" and others did their fair share of whispering. I felt bad for this man and his wife.

29. When should a man remove his hat?

 Answers will vary-see how many from this list are given:

- Upon entering a home
- At mealtime
- When being introduced to someone
- In a house of worship (unless the hat is part of a religious practice)
- In offices
- In restaurants
- In schools
- In libraries
- At funerals and weddings
- During movie or theater performances
- In courthouses
- When the United States flag passes by
- During the Pledge of Allegiance and national anthem

 Hats should definitely be removed indoors at mealtime. I suggest also removing when eating outside at a table, although there doesn't seem to be a clear rule on this. Use the lead of the host or elders in the group as a benchmark.

The hat is briefly removed or raised as a sign of respect in the presence of a lady, a superior or dignitary, in the presence of a passing funeral procession, or when passing a church. And don't think that the type of hat changes the rules — *baseball hats are still hats and do not get an exemption.*

Keep a hat clean at all times and avoid showing the inside of any style of hat. Etiquette dictates that a man does *not* need to remove a hat indoors if it is a public building (e.g., post office, airport, public transportation station, hotel lobbies). The hat may remain on in elevators and at athletic events (unless the national anthem is being played).[4] And although it may seem less relevant today, it is easier for a teen to just get in the habit now of removing a hat indoors and be sure he is not offending anyone. This is a controversial and complicated issue, but if there is any doubt, take it off!

30. When should a woman remove her hat?

 Under the same circumstances as a man (see above)

There are fewer rules for women when it comes to removing a hat *if* the hat is part of a particular outfit (meaning the hat cannot be worn with a variety of apparel). If the hat is worn in a man-like style (e.g., baseball hat, beanie, etc.), then she should apply the same rules. It is always a good idea to use common sense and follow the lead of those around.

> N *A women never tips or "doffs" her hat, like a man would do.*

 31. Describe what is meant by "good hygiene."

> N *Cancer patients with hair loss may wear a hat at all times, if they so choose.*

 Answers will vary, but should reference the appropriate level of cleanliness and appearance of a person

Let this discussion go where it needs to between adults and teens, but emphasize the importance of good hygiene (and grooming) as a

---

4 http://emilypost.com/advice/hats-off-hat-etiquette-for-everyone/

statement of how a person presents to the world. Personal appearance says a lot about how one feels about themselves and conveys the willingness to put forth extra effort to be pleasing to those around. Teenagers need to know that a person only gets one chance to make a good first impression and hygiene is a big part of that.

32. Name a minimum of 3 practices that contribute to "good hygiene."

Here is a list of possible answers, but give credit for any reasonable idea given:
- Cleaning nails
- Manicuring/trimming nails
- Daily showering or bathing
- Washing and styling hair
- Combing/brushing hair
- Grooming beards and moustaches
  - Trimming nose, eyebrow, and ear hair
  - Removing old make-up
  - Brushing and flossing teeth
  - Using deodorant
  - Wearing clean clothes

Clothing in good repair makes the best impression and requires garments to be wrinkle-free, absent of stains, have no missing buttons, no holes, hemmed pants that are not dragging on the ground, and be sized to fit the body.

Hygiene is a single word basically meaning "activities for preserving health." Taking care of the body on the inside and outside is a form of personal etiquette that reduces judgments and making others feel uncomfortable. You know what I am talking about. It's embarrassing to be with someone

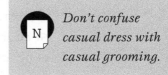
who obviously forgot their deodorant, has greasy hair, chews on their moustache, or has a hole in their pants allowing private parts to show. (Yikes!) Good hygiene is a *daily* fact of life.

> N *Don't confuse casual dress with casual grooming.*

Claire sat on her bed with the roll of masking tape and her new jeans. When her roommate Kathy inquired about what she was doing, Claire told her she was hemming her pants. Kathy chuckled and volunteered to get some thread. Claire said masking tape hems were easier than sewing hems and no one could see it, so she did it all the time.

"It sometimes comes off, but who cares. I'll just reapply more tape after the jeans get washed," she said while shrugging her shoulders.

Kathy shook her head in disbelief and walked away assuming Claire also used safety pins to reattach buttons that fell off.

33. List a minimum of 5 activities, related to bodily functions and grooming, that should not be done in the presence of another person.

> Here is a list of possible answers, but give credit for any reasonable replies:
> - Spitting
> - Scratching (especially in "private" areas)
> - Farting
> - Burping or belching
> - Popping zits (yours or anyone else's)
> - Picking your nose, toes, scabs, blisters, peeling sun burnt skin, etc.
> - Cracking knuckles

- Cracking, smacking, blowing bubbles, or chewing gum with your mouth open
- Sneezing or coughing without covering nose or mouth
- Flossing
- Leaving used tissues laying around
- Biting, cleaning, or cutting nails
- Brushing or combing hair
- Applying make-up (including lipstick)
- Shaving
- Peeling nail polish
- Chewing on hair
  - Picking wedgies
  - Excessive throat clearing
  - Excessive sniffling

The standard practice today is to cough or sneeze into your bent arm, at the elbow (turning your face away from those standing in front of you). This is to prevent germs from going directly towards others or onto a hand that may come into contact with other hands and objects before being washed.

Let's be honest and admit that many of the above behaviors happen at home with family and close friends, on occasion (or at least I hope it is *only* occasionally). And it is not the end of the world when it does happen. However, general courtesy dictates that individuals refrain from these behaviors in public as they are often unsanitary, offensive to others, and avoidable.

34. If someone is wearing too much perfume or cologne, how should you handle it?

⑨ Compliment first, then tell the person it may be a tiny bit too much

Most people, including teenagers, would not say anything in this situation (but then talk behind the person's back about it). The fear of hurting another person's feelings tends to keep us silent and a conversation like this is hard (no doubt). However, I would want to know if I applied too much perfume (especially if it was bothersome to a friend, family member, or colleague), wouldn't you? If you think of this scenario in those terms, politely mentioning the problem is actually doing someone a favor.

 Body sprays, lotions, deodorants, and even plug-in room deodorizers and diffusers can bother some people. Remember that more is not always better.

I suggest in the workplace, a friend should approach the fragrant one to lessen the blow (not a supervisor — too threatening).

35. After using the toilet, what 3 things should be done?

⑨ Put toilet seat and lid down, flush, wash your hands

Two additional polite gestures related to using the bathroom include wiping up water dripped on the countertop and closing the bathroom door. You can do more research and read about other similar practices under the topic of "Feng Shui Rules" on the internet. It is interesting stuff!

I want to leave this chapter with two additional concepts relating to things one can do on a personal level — understanding the "value of time" and "asking for help." At first, you may not see how these fit into *Personal Guidelines*, but think about it. Time is valuable (more so as you age-LOL). Respecting another person's time is a *courtesy* not to be overlooked. (I learned from a friend a long time ago that "on time … is late.") And asking for help is not a sign of weakness, but rather a sign of humility. Asking can be a time saver as well as a compliment to another person — it shows you regard them as an authority and value their input (just don't overdo it out of laziness).

Good role models allow the younger generation to see that living with manners, etiquette, and courtesy is a small price to pay to eliminate the risk of offending others with rude actions or appearing uninformed. Maybe humans should take a lesson from the animal population. Animals *adapt* to their environment to survive and *adopt behavior* accepted by their species. As a human being, social rules exist no matter what tribe or clique you belong to, so I encourage teenagers to *adapt and adopt.*

Remember that buying jeans with holes, wearing pants that ride low (with no belt to hold them up), tattoos, piercings, and not wearing panty hose are all forms of fads. Fads are temporary. Think back to the fluorescent/neon colors of the 90s, the big hair of the 80s, bell bottom pants of the 70s, and how their popularity passed...so LET IT GO! Just so young people know when to alter their normal clothing and the potential consequences for their choices in the short and long-term.

Additionally, hat etiquette is a pet peeve for many (including me), so judgments may be placed on someone who doesn't show respect and remove a hat. However, in today's world, hats are worn as part of a fashion statement to show a particular attitude or an affiliation to something. Hats are more than a protective garment and if not removing a hat at the proper time or place is the biggest etiquette faux pas a teen makes, mention it kindly and then...LET IT GO!

⑦ Dining Protocol

Assume U.S. practices for all questions.

1. Identify the following pieces you would find on a properly set table.

2. When dining at a restaurant, guests may arrive at different times. When should you take your seat at the table?

3. When invited to dinner at a home or restaurant, how do you know where to sit?

4. Should a man always pull a dining chair out for a woman?

5. Where should a woman place her purse once seated at the table?

6. Where should a man or woman place his/her briefcase once seated at the table?

7. After being seated and greeting others at the table, what is the first thing you should do?

8. How does one signal a waiter when ready to order?

9. Discuss steps taken to give a "toast" at a function (including what to say).

10. How do you know when it is OK to start eating your meal in a restaurant? What about in a home?

11. How do you know which glasses and plates are yours and not your neighbors at the table?

12. What is the rule to remember when deciding which piece of silverware to use? (i.e., Which fork first?)

13. When eating "American" style, how do you hold your fork and knife?

14. When eating "Continental" style, how do you hold your fork and knife?

15. Where do you place your fork when it is not in your hand? What about your knife and spoon?

16. How do you indicate you are finished with a course of a meal and you are ready for the next course?

17. What do you say when you need to leave the table during a meal?

18. If you must leave during a meal, where should you place your napkin?

19. Is it proper to cut all food first or should you cut and eat as you go?

20. Is it OK to combine food on the fork? (e.g., bite of meat with mashed potato)

21. When passing food to someone at the table, which way should you pass the dish-to the left or right?

22. What is the rule about using and passing salt and pepper?

23. When choosing butter, spreads, or dips from a table serving dish, what are the rules about using them?

24. If you have food allergies or dietary restraints and are eating outside of your own home, what do you need to do and when?

25. What do you do if you can't swallow a food product (e.g., gristle, bone, etc.)?

26. When eating soup, do you scoop towards or away from your body?

27. When not at home, is it polite to ask for a second helping?

28. Name 3 foods you may eat using your fingers.

29. Is it OK to lick your fingers?

30. What does a man need to do when a woman stands to leave the dining table?

31. Name one proper way to get a server's attention in a restaurant.

32. Where do you place your napkin when finished with a meal?

33. In a business setting, who should pay the dining bill, the person who extends the invitation or the guest?

34. With friends and family, who should pay the dining bill?

35. If you have a coupon or discount to be applied to a restaurant bill, should the tip be calculated before or after the reduction is taken?

36. If you don't finish your meal, is it OK to ask for a doggy bag or to-go box?

37. What is a "thank you note"?

38. Are thank you notes expected after having a dinner with someone? .

Misc. Vocab - Define the following dining related words...

39. Maître d' (mey-ter dee)
40. Sommelier (suhm-uh l-yey)
41. Hors d'oeuvres (or-derves)
42. Appetizer (ap-i-tahy-zer)
43. À la carte (ah luh kahrt)
44. Entrée (ahn-trey)
45. Buffet (buhf-it)
46. Flambé (flahm-bey)
47. En brochette (ahn-bro-shett)
48. Cutlery (kuht-luh-ree)
49. Sorbet (sawr-bey)
50. Condiment (kon-duh-muh nt)
51. Bon Appétit (baw na-pey-tee)
52. House Wine
53. Vintage (vin-tij)
54. Bistro (bis-troh)
55. Family Style Dining
56. Fine Dining

⑨ Dining Protocol

If you reviewed the *Dining Protocol* questions, you probably noticed that the list excluded several topics that you expected to see. I am choosing to call these "the obvious protocol" and I am taking the liberty of assuming children, from a very young age, are instructed to use these manners while dining. These lessons include:

1. no chewing with your mouth open
2. no elbows on the table, no leaning back on the chair, no fidgeting
3. no playing with or double dipping food
4. no slurping or smacking food
5. no gum in your mouth at the table
6. no reaching across the table — ask for food to be passed
7. no eating off the serving spoon or with your fingers
8. no hunching or slouching toward the plate — bring food to your mouth

Any of these ring a bell? What about eat slowly and enjoy your food? And of course, let's not forget adult figures insisting on the use of "please," "thank you," "may I —," etc. at the table. All good advice, but my focus in this section goes beyond these basic etiquette points. Let's first talk truth and consequences of *Dining Protocol*.

TC The first formal dining experience for teens can be intimidating. It can be daunting to suddenly be faced with eating unfamiliar foods (without making a face), a crowded table setting (not food in a bag), and an expectation to converse (not play on a cell phone). Many young people don't know why there is more than

Sports, movies, and upcoming social events are usually safe conversation topics. Avoid gossip about others not in attendance, sad stories, politics, religion, finances, and bad news.

one fork at a place setting. They can be perplexed when confronted with reaching to the left or right of the plate to access "their glass" and may immediately "dig in" not knowing the guidelines for when a person should start enjoying the meal.

I think that eating in front of the TV, in the car, and on the run has led to a generation that hasn't had opportunities to become adept at table/meal etiquette. Many teenagers simply believe they will never need to know this "dining stuff" and do not seek the knowledge — and maybe they are right. I, of course, still contend that knowing and practicing certainly doesn't hurt … just in case.

To be fair, teens today haven't practiced dining skills from an early age like previous generations. Etiquette has not been taught in schools since the 1960s and since this teaching has not transitioned consistently to the home, some apprehension is normal. Additionally, I think many people rarely sit down at a table together anymore and if they do, things are very casual (I admit my house is at times). Think — when was the last time you sat at a "set table" for a meal? (That long ago? Wow! It's been that long ago for me too!)

Have you noticed that some of the finer restaurants have changed their table settings to only include one fork, knife, and spoon at a time? Yep, I think they gave up on guests knowing which utensil to use when, so silverware is removed with each course of food and replacement flatware arrives with the next course to avoid patrons being confused. Watch for it!

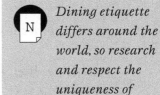
With what seems to be a decrease in formal dining today, teens can't take all the heat for not knowing or using good etiquette. However, as a teenager gets older (and certainly upon entering the adult workplace), they will be expected to use the rules of their culture. Since teens may resist dining etiquette rules, a reminder that all rules have a purpose can help. For example, rules when driving promote safety. Grammar rules create clarity. And rules for dining are so everyone will enjoy the process of eating together. (Makes more sense now, huh?)

> **N** *Dining etiquette differs around the world, so research and respect the uniqueness of different cultures.*

Protocol errors can cause embarrassment, anxiety, and fear with a deep and lasting effect on confidence levels. Using the wrong spoon, dropping food out of an open mouth, or drinking from someone else's water glass can have a negative, long lasting impression on everyone at the table. For centuries, American culture has placed importance on sharing a meal with others, so let's get prepared to continue the "breaking of bread" tradition and start with a question about place settings on a table.

Here's What A Teen Needs To Know...

Assume U.S. practices for all questions.

I. Identify the following pieces you would find on a properly set table.

A. NAPKIN
B. SERVICE PLATE
C. SOUP BOWL
D. BREAD PLATE & KNIFE
E. WATER GLASS
F. RED WINE GLASS
G. WHITE WINE GLASS
H. COFFEE/TEA CUP
I. SALAD FORK
J. FISH FORK
K. DINNER/ENTREE FORK (the biggest fork always)
L. GENERAL SERVICE KNIFE (for cutting soft things)

M. STEAK KNIFE

N. FISH KNIFE

O. SOUP SPOON

P. DESSERT SPOON &/OR FORK

Q. PLACECARD

By the time a child gets to double digits in age, they should be able to set a basic table with a napkin, fork, knife, spoon, plate, glass, and have each placed in the correct

Knife edges face plate.

position. As an individual approaches their twenties, the more complex formal setting (like the one pictured) should be part of a person's knowledge to set and use (regardless of economic standing). Being able to set a table properly allows others to benefit from the dining experience and demonstrates someone cared enough to put forth the best table presentation and use of table guidelines.

When I was first married, I was invited to a "Welcome Dinner" in honor of my husband because he had just accepted a new job. We got all dressed up and arrived at the restaurant 10 minutes early and after introductions (there were 10 other people), the maître d´ escorted us to the table.

I sat down, put my napkin on my lap, and accepted the menu from the waiter who had just introduced himself. As I glanced up and looked around the table, I froze. I was overwhelmed by all the utensils and glasses.

I leaned over to Tom and whispered, "I think I am out of my element here. I don't know what to order, yet alone which fork to eat it with."

He patted my knee under the table and gave me a smile to let me know it would be all right. I smiled back and decided to pattern my behavior after everyone else.

I still fondly remember that evening and although this girl from the suburbs of Pittsburgh never planned or expected to be dining at a restaurant of this caliber ... I survived and learned a lot to use going forward.

I suggest taking turns setting the table at home (at least occasionally). It's not really a "chore," just a part of the responsibilities for living in the house and a way to sneak in some practice for the future (and everyone will be learning more than table settings, trust me).

About ten years ago, my niece Vicki was asked to set the table for Thanksgiving dinner. We had 14 people dining and all the adults were busy in the kitchen. The next thing I know, I hear my daughter and her arguing. Apparently Leah had passed by and noticed the napkins were on the right side of the plate, all the silverware was placed on top of the napkin, and the glasses sat above the plate towards the left. Leah, being 4 years older, took it upon herself to start re-doing Vicki's work.

Vicki yelled, "Hey! What are you doing? I'm setting the table!"

Leah retaliated with, "Good grief — at your age, you should know how to set a table right!"

Hosts/hostesses will sometimes create 3-D figures or use a special folding pattern with a napkin before putting it on the table. In this case, placing the napkin on the plate is appropriate.

"You think you know it all," offended Vicki replied.

"Well, I certainly know the napkin goes left of the plate you idiot!"

With that, Vicki threw the remaining silverware in the center of the table and stormed off. Leah yelled after her, but Vicki just slammed the bedroom door shut.

Ten minutes later, I gathered both girls and the three of us finished the table. (We also spent some time talking about using kind words between cousins.)

2. When dining at a restaurant, guests may arrive at different times. When should you take your seat at the table?

> 🔑 Once a second person arrives-the others may join you at the table from there

> N *Some restaurants will not seat a party until everyone has arrived, so be courteous and arrive on time.*

3. When invited to dinner at a home or restaurant, how do you know where to sit?

> 🔑 You don't, so wait for instructions from the host/hostess

> N *The seat to the right of the host/hostess is a place of honor typically.*

Since it is the job of the host or hostess to create congenial conversation and provide a comfortable atmosphere for all, he or she might request guests sit in a pre-determined seat. Often place cards (or name cards) are used to label these place settings and put above or on the plate. This practice can occur in a restaurant, a banquet hall, or in a home setting.

> N *Remember to wash hands before approaching the table.*

If no card is used, wait and let the party giver inform guests *where* to sit or *when* to sit. It is also acceptable to ask the host/hostess where they would like you to sit. Teens need not be surprised if it is announced to "sit wherever you would like" as that is most common with informal dining events.

> N *A good rule of thumb is to seat "lefties" on the corner of a table to allow more freedom of movement for all.*

When in a restaurant, the server usually decides who will start the ordering so just follow that lead. If they do not, defer to women or the person to the right of the host to start the ordering. The host orders last unless doing the ordering for everyone.

Today, teenagers are aware that customs like pulling out a chair for a woman are not the norm. My advice is "expect less, but when courtesy comes, know it will be remembered." Something for both genders to ponder.

I advise teens never to just "plop down" before being invited to do so, as they may be asked to move, creating an uncomfortable situation. Men should help the women placed to their right side be seated (i.e., pull out the chair) and once all women are in chairs, the men may join them. In business, women are on their own for chair handling — that's life!

4. Should a man always pull a dining chair out for a woman?

In social settings, the majority do—in business, no

I suggest teens look around and take the lead from others on this one. Different customs may be the norm in a region, within a particular company, in certain homes, or within different age groups. Also, be aware of the female reaction. A guy can always back off if the body language and facial expression says, "I got it buddy!"

5. **Where should a woman place her purse once seated at the table?**

🔑 A small purse (evening bag size) can be placed behind the body on the chair (in the small of the back) or on the lap under the napkin—larger handbags (typically carried during the day) can be placed on an empty chair or on the floor to the left side

Ladies should make sure a purse is under the table or their chair to avoid anyone tripping. *Never put a purse on a table* (I won't even talk about all the nasty places that purse might have been previously — use your imagination) and avoid hanging it on the back of the chair. Hanging a purse on the back of a chair makes it easy to steal and it usually ends up on the floor anyway. Hanging from a "purse hook" is a relatively new idea that gals may like to try.

6. **Where should a man or woman place his/her briefcase once seated at the table?**

🔑 A briefcase always goes on the floor beside you

One last thought on handbags and briefcases — always present a clean bag, inside and out. A person can't be put together on the outside, then open a purse or briefcase to grab something and have disorganization. Old tissues, crumpled receipts, random papers, and candy wrappers popping out everywhere will reveal a lot, as will a tote

In a restaurant, a coat or jacket can be placed on an empty chair or the back of your chair if there is no coatroom area.

that is worn looking on the outside. If money is loose and just thrown inside, others may believe the bag owner lacks financial responsibility, and that could take away from an overall good impression. (Of course, I am assuming that organization *is* a valued trait by the majority of people.) An additional item that is *never placed on the tabletop is a cell phone!!!*

Tyrone, Darnell, and Maurice were having dinner over at Dominique's house. Basketball practice had made the boys hungry and ready to chow down. They ran through the door and directly to the kitchen table while sniffing to gather hints about what Mrs. Carter was making for dinner.

"Hey Dominique. I love your mom for having us for dinner, but this big bowl on the table is empty. What's with that?" Tyrone exclaimed just as Mrs. Carter entered the room and spoke.

"Well men. I will tell you all right now. That is the cell phone bowl. See, in order to eat in this house, you must place your cell phone in this bowl till after dinner. I won't be having any electronic disruptions that distract you from enjoying each other and my fine cookin'."

Mrs. Carter picked up the bowl, smiled, and approached each of the guys one at a time. Darnell started to say something and then grinned as he reached into his pocket. Maurice tossed his phone in the bowl and announced, "That's cool, but what is for dinner, ma'am? I could eat this phone!"

7. After being seated and greeting others at the table, what is the first thing you should do?

Put your napkin on your lap

A cue in a formal setting to pick up your own napkin is when you see the host/hostess do so. In an "upscale" restaurant, the server will open everyone's napkin and place it on laps, so be ready. Otherwise, you are on your own to tend to the napkin upon taking your seat.

Place napkin ring to the left of the plate once the napkin is removed.

Since napkins come in various sizes, teens should know that a large napkin stays folded in half and is placed on a lap. A small napkin should be opened all the way before placing over the upper legs. I would say that what constitutes a "large" and "small" napkin is a judgment call. After all, a petite

If a napkin is dropped on the floor, pick it up. It is then your choice to use it or ask for a replacement.

female may always need to fold the napkin as her lap is tiny and a 6' 5" man would always open a napkin fully. Just so no one snaps a napkin open or tucks a napkin into their shirt! (OK ... tucking napkins or using a provided "bib" *may* be allowed in certain venues to protect clothing while eating lobster, BBQ, or other messy food items. Just make sure the majority of patrons are doing it!)

8. **How does one signal a waiter when ready to order?**

 Close the menu

Since teens are still working on the skill of patience (as we all are), I want them to realize that after 15 minutes of waiting, one can order if someone is late (seems like a good time to mention this point). A quick telephone call to update a dining companion when running behind is expected, but things do happen so feel free to order at the 15-minute mark. It is only fair, especially to the restaurant staff.

If sharing an entree or dessert, ask for a second plate. Do not eat off another person's plate — not even a taste, they say!

Another ordering protocol for teens to learn is to order a middle priced entree and/or follow the lead of the host when you are a guest. Ordering the surf and turf may come off as pretentious and ordering a side salad may look skimpy, regardless of who is paying.

 9. Discuss steps taken to give a "toast" at a function (including what to say).

 Answers will vary

Giving a toast is a way to share feelings and/or gratitude to a group, host or hostess, or honoree and can be approached in a variety of ways. However, learning a generic, basic toast regiment will get a teen started on this dining tradition and the skill can develop over time.

 Giving a toast:

- Choose appropriate time and stand
- Raise your glass into the air while saying, "I'd like to make a toast."
- Pause as others retrieve their glass and stop conversations
- Give toast (e.g., "Cheers!" "To us!" "To the hostess." "Here's to the employee of the month, John.")
- Move your glass toward the center of the table (other guests should follow suit)

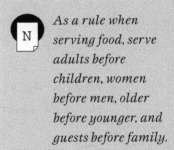
→ Touch your glass lightly to other guest's glasses (touch everyone's glass that can be reached without straining)

→ Sip your beverage and replace glass on table as you sit down

N *If a person gives a lengthy toast, know that each subsequent toast should get shorter and the overall number needs to be limited.*

10. **How do you know when it is OK to start eating your meal in a restaurant? What about in a home?**

(?) Rule is the same regardless of place - after everyone has been served and/or when the host/hostess starts to eat

I'd like to mention that food, especially in a restaurant, is often served sporadically. Because this food could get cold, those *who have not been served may instruct others to start enjoying before the last plate is brought to the table.* Otherwise, one should not even take a nibble before everyone has his/her dish, but you may enjoy your beverage.

N *As a rule when serving food, serve adults before children, women before men, older before younger, and guests before family.*

11. **How do you know which glasses and plates are yours and not your neighbors at the table?**

(?) Glasses are to the right of the plate, above the knife - bread plates are to the left, above the fork

The water glass is closest to the center of the plate and usually the largest in size. Wine glasses are placed to the right of the water with red wine in the middle (think WRW — water, red wine, white wine).

Just say "no thank you" if offered a beverage you do not want. Do not place a hand over the glass.

 Here are two sure fire ways to remember what is where:

→ Make "OK" signs with both of your hands like this

→ The left hand makes the letter "b" for "bread" (bread is on the left side)
→ The right hand makes the letter "d" for "drinks" (drinks are on the right side)

OR

→ Think "BMW" — starting to the left and going to the right (like you read), you have your bread (B), meal (M), and water (W)

12. What is the rule to remember when deciding which piece of silverware to use? (i.e., Which fork first?)

 Always use the outer most utensil first and work inward towards the plate with each course served-the rule is simply "out to in"

 Remember if any of the silverware is dirty, discreetly ask the server or host to replace it or just don't use it. Don't try to clean it yourself or make a fuss.

13. When eating "American" style, how do you hold your fork and knife?

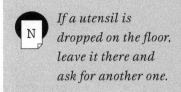

N If a utensil is dropped on the floor, leave it there and ask for another one.

⑨ Hold your fork with your dominant hand like you do a pencil (with the handle between thumb and index/middle fingers) and allow the tines to face upward as you pick up food to put in your mouth—the knife is placed across the top of the plate with the blade facing inward until needed

American style eating involves a lot of switching the fork and knife back and forth between the dominant and non-dominant hand because you always use your dominant hand to "do the work." Let me explain... if a person is cutting food, the fork moves to the non-dominant hand and the knife is removed from the plate by the dominant hand to "do the work of cutting." The knife handle is cupped in the palm, so the fingers and thumb can be wrapped around the handle for security. The cutting side of the knife faces downward as the fork (tines down) holds the item to be cut (similar to the continental style). Once the item is cut, the knife is placed back on the plate and the fork is shifted to the dominant hand (tines facing up and ready to "do the work") and the food is eaten.

14. When eating "Continental" style, how do you hold your fork and knife?

⑨ Hold the fork in the left hand with tines facing down and hold the knife in the right hand with your

 index finger along the top of the blade (wrapping all other fingers and the thumb around the handle)-use the fork to spear food and eat while keeping the tines facing down and in the same hand

 Procedures can be reversed if a person is left handed.

Continental style is most commonly seen in western Eurpeon countries, but anyone can use it. The important thing to remember is to *pick one style and stick with it*. Don't alternate between the two styles.

15. Where do you place your fork when it is not in your hand? What about your knife and spoon?

All silverware goes on the edge of the plate, making sure no part of the silverware touches the table-the knife handle is placed at the one o'clock position with the sharp edge turned inward

and pointing to the twelve o'clock position-the fork goes at the four o'clock position, tines upward and a spoon (if you have one) rests on the cup saucer (a spoon isn't used for an entree and doesn't go on the entree plate)

 Same goes for chop sticks. Chop sticks should be placed on a plate and never touch the table.

16. How do you indicate you are finished with a course of a meal and you are ready for the next course?

⑨ Place the knife and fork parallel with the handles in the four o'clock position and the tips in the ten o'clock position - the knife blade faces inward - use the same placement when the meal is complete

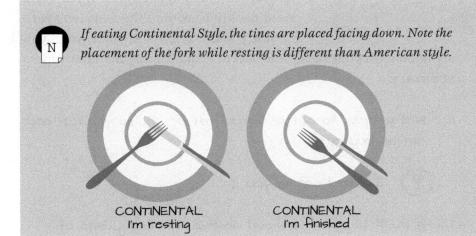

If eating Continental Style, the tines are placed facing down. Note the placement of the fork while resting is different than American style.

CONTINENTAL
I'm resting

CONTINENTAL
I'm finished

17. What do you say when you need to leave the table during a meal?

⑨ "Excuse me"

There is no need to make an announcement of why you are leaving the table. Needing to use the restroom, blow a nose, or make a phone call isn't anyone's concern.

In upscale establishments, the waitperson or their assistant will often refold your napkin and place it on the table or bring you a completely new napkin. Be aware and go with the flow.

18. If you must leave during a meal, where should you place your napkin?

(?) **Place your napkin on your chair** (hiding the heavily soiled area)

Don't place it on the back of the chair as it is easily seen and may fall off. Some sources say to put the napkin loosely to the left of your plate. However, placing a used napkin back onto the table isn't very sanitary and may give the impression you are done with your meal. It is best to avoid leaving the table unless necessary.

19. Is it proper to cut all food first or should you cut and eat as you go?

(?) Cut and eat as you go

20. Is it OK to combine food on the fork? (e.g., bite of meat with mashed potato)

(?) No

Many individuals like the taste created when different food flavors are mixed and would debate my answer to this question. However, the "experts" say this shouldn't be done and so I suggest not doing it (especially when dining with others). I believe that casseroles were invented by those who like flavors blended and I definitely support cooking and eating those!

> When asked to pass something (e.g., salt/pepper, butter, side dish), do not use it first. They asked first, so pass it first.

21. **When passing food to someone at the table, which way should you pass the dish-to the left or right?**

    🔑 **To the right** (counter clockwise)

Remember to hold the dish for the person on your right so they can serve themselves before taking possession of the dish. This helps alleviate spills and allows your neighbor to lift a lid with one hand and serve himself with the other (a nice gesture).

22. **What is the rule about using and passing salt and pepper?**

    🔑 **Never use without tasting first and pass salt and pepper together** (even if only one was requested)

Let's all get into the habit of tasting food before applying salt and pepper to be sure additional seasoning is needed. It would be so easy to insult the chef by altering food with seasoning, so try to avoid adding ingredients if possible (depending on the item, this advice would include condiments).

Joley bought four filet mignons and asked cousins, Linda and Mark, to come over for dinner on Saturday night. Joley worked all day in the kitchen and had prepared a fabulous meal with twice baked potatoes, green beans, and cheesecake for dessert. Matt grilled the steaks to perfection and the foursome sat down to eat.

"Hey Joley. Can I get some ketchup?"

"For what?"

"For my steak, of course."

"Are you kidding me? I spent $14.99 a pound on these steaks, Matt seasoned and cooked them with love, and you want to drown them in ketchup! You haven't even tasted yours yet."

"I don't have to taste mine. I like ketchup on everything." Linda said as she rose to get ketchup from the refrigerator herself.

"Wow! Didn't know that about you. Remind me to make hamburgers next time," Joley replied with a smile.

23. **When choosing butter, spreads, or dips from a table serving dish, what are the rules about using them?**

> Take a sampling and place it on your bread plate with the serving utensil provided - use your personal knife to apply butter, spread, or dip to the bread or cracker prior to each bite (not to the whole item at one time).

As I speak of eating bread with a meal, I must share a story about my dear Grandma Rose. I can still hear her at meal time making this offer to me — "Here honey, have a piece of bread to use as a shovel!" It may sound shocking, but she knew her etiquette. A person can use bread to push food onto a fork! You can also use a knife as an aid, but do not use your fingers.

FYI — wiping a plate with bread to soak up sauces or butter is a no-no.

A 12-year old was eating with his mother at the local café. While she was busy enjoying her own meal, he picked up his cup of au jus juice and drank it instead of dipping his sandwich into the cup. She didn't notice until the server walked over and had to "set him straight." Kevin said he didn't know! Both mother and son were embarrassed and apologetic.

24. If you have food allergies or dietary restraints and are eating outside of your own home, what do you need to do and when?

> As soon as possible, inform the host throwing the dinner party of any items you cannot eat because of health reasons-if eating at a restaurant, go online or call the restaurant to check on their ability to meet dietary limitations

Alerting a hostess or host by telephone (rather than email or text) would be best as they may have questions about your health constraints that need discussion. And know that I am talking about giving advance notice on items that if eaten, would cause real health concerns. This may seem pushy or awkward, but remember that you have no control over allergies and limitations — a good host/hostess will want to make accommodations. If dining at a restaurant and you are not able to call in advance to inquire about limitations, ask your server to verify any concerns you might have before ordering your meal.

Please remember that it is not polite to call and give a list of things you "just don't like" or demand foods that correspond to your current "diet craze." I tell adolescents that "if you don't like a dish served or don't want to eat it because you are trying the newest fad diet, just don't eat it" — pass on that particular dish. There is no need to mention a dislike, make a face, or create a scene if something appears on the table that doesn't agree with your taste buds.

Omar and Missy arrived at the local Japanese restaurant for dinner. Missy knew that this would be an adventure since her Japanese host had planned to order each course of the meal to ensure the group would have an authentic Japanese experience. She took a deep breath and smiled as Osamu and Mitsuko greeted her inside the doorway.

Missy was starting to feel better about the evening as delightful conversation ensued, drinks were enjoyed, and the first course of the meal was over. Suddenly, the second round of plates were set on the table in front of Missy and she exclaimed, "I'm not eating this, it's creepy!" (the shrimp had tail, legs, and eyes still attached).

Luckily everyone just laughed.

If a person has something struck in their teeth, alert them as quietly as possible. They should not try to remove it while sitting at the table. The protocol is to excuse yourself and return after the problem has been solved.

25. What do you do if you can't swallow a food product (e.g., gristle, bone, etc.)?

Remove the food by placing your napkin in front of your mouth and sliding the food back onto your utensil

Basically, the rule is to remove the food the same way it went into the mouth. Once removed, place the food on the side of the plate and let it blend in with the other food as best as you can. Finger foods can be removed with fingers, like a fried chicken bone, just never spit it into your napkin. (How embarrassing would it be if that piece of gristle rolled onto the floor or created a grease spot on your pants?) And if you ever find yourself choking on food, stay at the table and point to your throat. This might seem inappropriate, but you may need real help from someone in your party.

26. **When eating soup, do you scoop towards or away from your body?**

⑨ Scoop away from your body

I know that in some cultures slurping and drinking directly from the soup bowl is expected, but not in the U.S. so don't do it! (Tacky!) There is a little rhyme my friend Sue taught me that may help you remember to properly eat soup—"Push the boat out to sea and then bring it back to me."

27. **When not at home, is it polite to ask for a second helping?**

⑨ Not at a formal event-wait to be offered more
(use judgment at informal events away from home)

28. **Name 3 foods you may eat using your fingers.**

⑨ Answers will vary, but here is a list of several items[5]:
- Fried chicken
- Crisp bacon
- Bread/roll
- Corn on the cob

---

5 http://chefalbrich.com/etiquette/proper_eat_fingers.htm

Damp cloths offered before (e.g., on an airplane) or after food (e.g., after eating crab legs) are to be unfolded, used to wipe hands only, and placed back on the tray.

- French fries/chips
- Whole fruit/fruit on the stem
- Hamburger/hot dog on a bun
- Sandwich
- Tacos (retrieving any food that escapes with fork)
- Artichoke
- Asparagus (provided it is not cooked in a dipping sauce)
- Hors d'oeuvres/canapés/crudités (almost everything pre-meal)
- Cookie
- Pizza
- Some sushi and seafood (e.g., crab legs would require hands and seafood utensils)

29. Is it OK to lick your fingers?

 No

30. What does a man need to do when a woman stands to leave the dining table?

 Rise until she walks away

If a woman stands, so should all the men at the table. May seem a little old school, but you can never go wrong with being too polite or courteous. It's an easy way to stand out (no pun intended) and make some brownie points with the group or a lady. (Plus, it's good for circulation!)

31. Name one proper way to get a server's attention in a restaurant.

Answers vary, but all of these are acceptable:
- Make eye contact with server
- Nod at server
- Raise a hand
- Raise an index finger
- Use server's name when they are close by

Fact is, humans like and will respond best when called by name (just like a dog will wag their tail wildly when you call out their name). Not that I am suggesting a server is in any way similar to a dog, but using a server's name will get better results than trying to get attention with "Miss" or "Sir." The rule of thumb is if a server introduces himself or herself by name, use it. Otherwise, "Miss" or "Sir" at least shows respect. I teach all these methods as one never knows which will work best in a given restaurant situation. Never clap, snap fingers, yell across the room, or say, "Hey you."

Dishes should be cleared from the right side of a person as food is served from the left side.

32. Where do you place your napkin when finished with a meal?

Loosely to the left of your plate without folding or wadding-if the plate has been removed, lay it where plate was (never place a linen napkin on a plate)

33. In a business setting, who should pay the dining bill, the person who extends the invitation or the guest?

 The person who does the inviting

If possible, tell the waiter in advance that you would like to receive the check. This will alleviate that awkward check grabbing struggle or evasive pause when no one claims the bill on the table. If everyone works for the same company and there is no established host, the highest ranking individual is responsible for paying the check.

34. With friends and family, who should pay the dining bill?

 It depends on the precedent you have set in previous situations

If your friend bought last time, you should pick up the tab this time. However, friends often split the check or get separate checks (called "going Dutch"). Family dynamics can be a crap-shoot. For example, if we go out with my mom and my husband is there, he pays. If it is just Mom and me, she pays because I'm the favorite daughter. (Did I mention I'm the only daughter?) And now that my children are grown, my husband and I pay with them offering to "buy" occasionally. (You should see their faces when we hand over the check!) Perhaps the best advice is to announce if you intend to pay when the dining out invitation is initiated. If that doesn't happen, then plan to at least pay your share.

The bill comes to the table. It lays there between the three brothers. Finally, Alex picks it up as Michael starts taking money from his pocket for the food he just ate. They both stop and look at Eric. Nothing.

No reaching for his wallet, no eye contact, and they don't hear, "Hey, let me pick up the tab today."

Frustrated again, Alex says, "Eric, you owe $14.00, plus tip."

"Oh, yeah. Got it."

Whether you are a teen or adult, don't be the person with a reach impediment — the cheap one. The one who always has to be dunned for money. *Keep track of the approximate cost of what is ordered (including appetizers and desserts) and don't forget to add in tax and a tip as you contribute to a bill.* Be forthcoming with payment when the check arrives.

I tell teenagers that the other option is to learn to ask for a separate check … which involves stating your preference when ordering. This ensures a person will not pay more than his/her fair share. However, let's be honest — paying a few extra dollars on a group tab isn't the end of the world. In the long run, it all evens out and the price is worth not getting the reputation of being the "tightwad" in the group.

35. If you have a coupon or discount to be applied to a restaurant bill, should the tip be calculated before or after the reduction is taken?

   (?) Calculate the tip on the original total price before any coupons or discounts

36. If you don't finish your meal, is it OK to ask for a doggy bag or to-go box?

   (?) Yes

Even fine restaurants support not wasting good food. However, on dates and in business settings an individual may want to forgo this practice. It can be awkward and be perceived as being needy.

Try to order a meal that corresponds in size to what can be enjoyed and consumed during that sitting. Consider if the food you take will need (and get) refrigeration before taking it (spoiling food in the car smells bad) and follow the protocol of others in the group.

37. What is a "thank you note"?

> Written correspondence that expresses gratitude from one person to another

38. Are thank you notes expected after having a dinner with someone?

> Probably not expected, but are a nice touch and will be remembered fondly

Teenagers often ask me, "Is a thank you note only sent when the other person pays?" I jokingly say, "Definitely, as they just saved you dough!" However, showing appreciation for the companionship and time together after *any* dining event is a sign of maturity and kindness. As discussed during the *General Etiquette* chapter, a hand-written note (written on a note card, stationery, or paper) has the most impact. However, a text or email is still better than no acknowledgement.

Misc. Vocab-Define the following dining related words...

39. Maitre d'

(9) Person who greets guests upon arrival in a restaurant and shows them to their table

40. Sommelier

(9) Waiter in charge of wines in a club or restaurant

41. Hors d'oeuvres

(9) Food items served before the main meal

Hors d'oeuvres is a French word that translates to mean "outside the meal" and are often served in smaller portions meant to be eaten with fingers and served prior to a meal. If attending a formal gathering, this food is often distributed by servers who circulate the room with trays (and small plates and/or napkins) while guests are arriving and mingling before dinner. During less formal functions, a table is typically provided for self-service hors d'oeuvres.

42. Appetizer

(9) Food served as the first course of a meal

Although the names are used interchangeably at times, an appetizer differs from a hors d'oeuvre because it is the first course of a meal and provided once a person is seated at the table. Appetizers are larger in size and a course of a meal like a dessert.

43. Á la carte

    Menu items individually priced

44. Entrée

    The main course of a meal

45. Buffet

    Self-serve tables of food

46. Flambé

    Flaming dish

47. En brochette

    On a skewer

48. Cutlery

    Tools for eating (another name for silverware or utensils)

49. Sorbet

    Flavored ice cream

During fine dining, sorbet is often used to cleanse the palate between courses. Teens can be unsure of why this traditional dessert item is being served out of order, so I included sorbet in the vocabulary list to bring that possibility to light.

50. Condiment

🔑 Something used to give a special flavor to food (mustard, ketchup, spices, etc.)

51. Bon Appétit

🔑 Means "good appetite" and used as a salutation just before eating

52. House Wine

🔑 Recommended wine of a particular restaurant

53. Vintage

🔑 Year and region where wine was made

54. Bistro

🔑 Small, European-style restaurant or café

N *If wine is being served and you are underage or not consuming, do not turn the glass over on the table. Just say, "No thank you."*

55. Family Style Dining

🔑 Presentation of food whereby serving dishes are placed on the table and everyone serves themselves

56. Fine Dining

 Very expensive eating establishment

 Additional dining vocabulary can be found at www.learninginfoforeveryday.com.

Family style is so much fun and allows diners to have a casual, home-like atmosphere. Some restaurants that specialize in this style of preparation and service may seat more than one party of guests together at a table and will expect sharing among all patrons. As you have probably already guessed, there is a set price for each customer, regardless of how much or how little you eat, so go hungry! (Typically, there is a reduced rate for children.)

///////////////////////

I'd like to close by being honest and admitting that in daily life, we all violate many of these dining decorum protocols and that isn't the end of the world. However, we shouldn't always eat the "way we want" any more than a person should drive on the wrong side of the road just because "they want to." Expectations exist in this aspect of life too.

Staying unsophisticated because of "not knowing" or claiming to "not care" when it comes to dining protocol is a cop-out. Not acknowledging that the opinions of others matter, whether you care or not, is arrogance no one can afford. Claiming good etiquette is a "snobbish or uppity" thing to do is just an excuse for not practicing appropriate manners. Teens will often say they don't have a career, an income level, or a desire to be around those who place value on formal dining — but this is really just another cop-out! If teens and adults do what they are supposed to do, at the right time, in the right places — they will survive and even thrive! Teenagers need to practice (on a regular basis) and put on an "Inside Eating Face" and an "Inside Manners Face" ... period! (Okay — I'm done preaching now!)

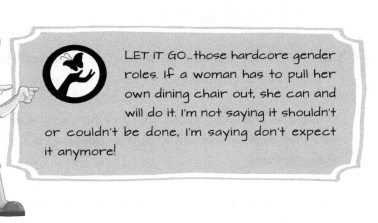

LET IT GO...those hardcore gender roles. If a woman has to pull her own dining chair out, she can and will do it. I'm not saying it shouldn't or couldn't be done, I'm saying don't expect it anymore!

⑦ Oral Communication

1. When greeting someone you know in person, what is a good opening line?

 2. Demonstrate how to introduce yourself to someone you do not know.

3. What are the five questions you can ask someone you just met which will result in getting to know them better?

4. What do you say when introducing one person to another?

5. What is the rule about whose name to state first in an introduction?

6. Define networking.

7. At what point is it OK to start calling an adult or older individual by their first name?

8. What do you do if you forget someone's name?

9. Define small talk.

10. When starting a conversation, should you use open ended or closed ended questions?

11. What are topics of conversation to discuss and avoid in a social setting?

12. When speaking with or to others, name any 5 good habits to apply. (Hint: can be physical or oral habits)

13. Define filler word (as it pertains to oral communication).

14. Name three words or phrases (called filler words) to avoid that people typically use without realizing it.

15. For good communication to occur, should a person listen more or speak more?

16. When giving a compliment, what should you always remember to do?

17. When receiving a compliment, what should you always remember?

18. When giving an apology, what should you always remember?

19. Explain the difference between a telephone landline and a cell phone line.

20. When placing a long distance call from a landline in the U.S., what does a person need to dial before the ten-digit telephone number? Why?

21. When calling a place of business, what are the first three pieces of information you should supply when someone answers?

22. When leaving a telephone message, what information should be included?

23. What is the proper way to answer a home telephone?

24. When taking a telephone message for someone else, what information should be included?

25. What is the acceptable length of time to put someone on hold?

Misc. Vocab-Define the following oral communication related terms...

26. Three-way Calling/Conferencing
27. Teleconferencing

28. How many feet should be between someone using a cell phone and another individual?

29. List five or more places where it is inappropriate to use your cell phone.

⑨ Oral Communication

Written and oral communication throughout time has gone from sketches in caves with grunting men to sophisticated linguistics transmitted over thousands of miles in a fraction of a second. The original use of plants and other items in nature to make ink and create inscriptive messages has evolved (thank goodness) and we now send communication via cyberspace with a simple key stroke or button push (scary as that is, at times). Man can talk across long distances to not only one other person, but also to groups and achieve visual contact at the same time. So, with all this change in communication, are teenagers really prepared and better off when it comes to social communication skills?

TC There seems to be much concern today about *young people losing the art of well-rounded interaction skills* because they prefer to rely on email, texting, and the internet exclusively (a valid point in my experience). Think about this ...

1. Many teens have never placed a telephone call to order an item or make an inquiry. They communicate strictly electronically (even when ordering a pizza).
2. Some adolescents have never written a letter using correct business format and struggle to address an envelope properly to mail a letter.
3. Many teenagers believe greeting someone or answering a telephone call by saying "Sup?" is as good as any other salutation. ("Sup?" means "What's up?" — in case you weren't sure.)

4. Most teens can run circles around adults when it comes to electronic skills, but hesitate with face-to-face dialogue.

Since good written *and* oral communication is a crucial skill in *both the workplace and in private life,* shouldn't we all take the time and energy to master the art of both forms of communication and ensure teens are confident in their skills?

I worry when adolescents tell me that they know "how" to talk to people when they "have to" and with the capabilities of the internet, their "need to" is limited. Can anyone really turn these skills and knowledge on and off like a light bulb? (I know I would struggle with that!) I contend that good communication cannot be limited to "on demand" performances. Communication must be learned and practiced with the same determination an athlete puts into perfecting his/her sport.

It has also been my observation that teenagers who lack solid communication skills are slower to respond to oral questions, struggle to think on their feet, and avoid written correspondence for fear of making mistakes. Weak communication leads to poorer grades in school, struggles with job applications and interviews, less frequent promotions at work, and bewilderment concerning career aspirations that are left unfulfilled.

Take a minute and think of adults that you know currently. Has the ability to use appropriate speaking, listening, and writing skills had an effect on anyone's standard of living? How are these individuals doing in their marital, sibling, work, and peer relationships? Do these friends and family members spend a lot of time being frustrated when they must use written and/or oral communication to solve work and personal issues? And I bet you know individuals who *do use first-rate communication skills* and you've noticed they are more successful as a result.

I've probably asked too many questions of you to ponder in this truth and consequence section, so let me just conclude with this thought... I hope you will join me in believing that teens need to care enough to speak and write clearly, with proper etiquette, so others will care enough to listen and read what he/she has to say. I will start with a discussion of oral communication and follow with written correspondence in the next chapter.

Here's What A Teen Needs To Know...

1. **When greeting someone you know in person, what is a good opening line?**

    (9) "Hi!" or "Hello"-followed by "How are you?" or "Nice to see you again."

A slightly different approach would be to say, "Good Morning" or "Good Afternoon," as applicable. Adding a person's name or bringing up a topic from the last conversation you had together will make them feel extra special, so I encourage it.

 2. **Demonstrate how to introduce yourself to someone you do not know.**

(9) Demonstrations will vary, but should include:
- Establishing eye contact with body language that shows approachability (smile, good posture, head up, etc.)
- Brief greeting (Hi or Hello) followed by providing first and last name (e.g., "Hi! I'm Beth Carey.")

- Inquiry about other person's name (e.g., "I'm Beth Carey and you are?")
- Exchange of pleasantry (e.g., "Nice to meet you.")
- Offering of a handshake

Remember that oral communication, like all social skills, is dependent on culture and tradition. Do research, be prepared, and follow the lead of others if there is any uncertainty.

If a person is representing a company at the time of an introduction, including the company name and a job title is acceptable as part of the interaction. This is also a good time to exchange business cards.

Introducing yourself is easy, although many teens fail to take the initiative. I say, "Just do it!" After all, an introduction can be as short as, "Hello. My name is Beth Carey. What is your name?" Add a handshake, a general comment, or a few kind words to simply acknowledge appreciation for the chance to meet and it is over. For example, a person could say, "Nice meeting you Andrea. This is a great party, huh?"

Follow-up conversation usually stems from there, but not always. To avoid awkward silence, one can always start by asking a question (see question 3 for some ideas). This shows interest in the other person and helps to avoid a lull during the encounter.

3. What are five questions you can ask someone you just met which will result in getting to know them better?

Answers will vary - these are my suggestions:

- "Where are you from originally?"
- "What brought you here?"-if they are not from the area you are in currently
  ~ If person is from your current area, ask-"Have you lived here all your life?"
- "Do you have a family?"
  ~ If a person is young, use-"Tell me about your family?"
- "What do you do for a living?"
  ~ If a person is younger, ask-"Are you a student or do you work?"
- "What did you want to be when you were growing up?"
  ~ If a person is young, use-"What do you want to be when you grow up?"[6]

These questions are what I like to call "safe questions." They can be used any time, in any circumstance, and by all ages. They work because they are non-threatening and informal, yet you get to know a person while making them feel special. You can use the information in a future conversation or as a connection to another person in an introduction. For example, you might have the opportunity to say, "Donna, this is Wanda and she moved here recently too!"

Asking questions allows you to control a conversation and keep it going. I want teens to remember the acronym MMFI (Make Me Feel Important)[7] when meeting new people. Typically individuals like to talk about themselves, so let them. After all, the goal is to have a relationship with someone and learning about them as a person is a good start.

---

6 www.BoazPower.com
7 www.BoazPower.com

4. **What do you say when introducing one person to another?**

Always introduce people by their preferential name (e.g., Robert likes being called Bob).

 Say "Name 1, this is Name 2" (e.g., "Liam, this is Isaac.")

5. **What is the rule about whose name to state first in an introduction?**

 Always say the name of the most important person first-say the higher-ranking name first out of respect as you are introducing the junior member to the senior (e.g., "Mom, this is my friend, Sam. Sam, this is my mom, Mrs. Pizzuto")

Introductions are important to make others feel comfortable, enable everyone to participate in the conversation, establish rapport, and to show respect (introductions are huge deals in most cultures and can't be overlooked). It is always wise to add the reason you want people to meet or a common connection for them so it is easier for people to relate to each other.

Here are the basic introduction scenarios and an example of what to say:

Younger to older	"Ms. King, this is my little brother, Matty."
Man to woman	"Keyshia, meet Jacob." (female name goes first unless there is a ranking consideration)
Lower ranking business associate to higher associate	"Mr. CEO, I would like you to meet Linda Lachman from accounting."

Associates with same rank	"Foster, I'd like you to meet the manager of the Detroit office, Kennedy Morgan." (you know Foster better because he is your boss, so his name goes first, even though he and Kennedy are equal in rank)
Group to individuals	"Joe and Janet, I'd like to introduce Barb, Rosie, Bill and John."
Person to relative	"Aunt Joan, this is my roommate, Damarco."

6. Define networking.

Connection or interaction between people that is developed to enhance one's relationships

Networking is a term most often associated with the connections made that enhance one's career (although it is done in all walks of life). Teenagers should start learning the importance of networking early as *who you know can be as important, if not more important, than what you know* and it starts with introductions.

7. At what point is it OK to start calling an adult or older individual by their first name?

When he or she invites you to do so-use their title (Mr./Mrs./Ms./Dr./Reverend/Father) **and last name until told otherwise**

Did you know that this etiquette point applies to adults too? Somewhat surprising that such a formality holds true for all ages, but titles can be a big deal in many cultures, regions, situations, and with certain individuals. Better to play it safe and wait for the invitation to be less formal and use a given name.

8. What do you do if you forget someone's name?

    (?) Be upfront and admit you forgot the name

Everyone has lapses in memory (more as you age, I must admit). Teens can be taught to simply say, "I'm sorry, but I have forgotten your name," or "I know we have met before, but I'm afraid I've forgotten your name." Saying your own name can sometimes lead to the other person giving theirs, but there is no guarantee of that so I tell teens to just own it and move on. (Be cognizant of others struggling to recall you own name and supply it.)

9. Define small talk.

    (?) Informal discussion, having little purpose, covering no specific topic

Small talk is conversation for the sake of talking. It is often used with a new acquaintance or someone you don't know well. It helps to fill that awkward silence and is usually short in nature. However, it is an important social skill to develop.

10. When starting a conversation, should you use open ended or closed ended questions?

    (?) Open ended questions

Open ended questions can have an infinite number of answers, so they are best to use when starting a conversation with someone. (e.g., Where were you born?) The response to closed ended questions typically elicit a yes or no reply. (e.g., Where you born in Atlanta?)

Using open ended questions encourages a conversation to take a variety of paths and allows others to move the conversation to topics that they enjoy talking about.

II. **What are topics of conversation to discuss and avoid in a social setting?**

Here is a list of possible answers, but use judgment when accepting responses:

AVOID
- Politics
- Religion
- Gossip
- Topics that tend to be sad or have bad news (e.g., surgery, sick pet)
- Gory or gruesome stories
- Disparaging ethnic, racial, or religious jokes
- Money matters

DISCUSS
- Sports
- Weather
- Music/movies/TV shows
- Upcoming community events
- Family (i.e., number of siblings, who lives where, etc.)
- Where you live
- Career/job/school

THINK, then speak. Teenagers often have regrets (as do adults) for not thinking through a concept before blurting it out. Bragging about the undefeated football record of your team with someone who has allegiance to a rival never works.

Starting and engaging in a conversation can be difficult at any age, so it is nice when teens are ready with safe and prepared conversation topics to ease stress. Throw in some nervousness about using other proper etiquette behaviors and soon young people will gravitate to electronics rather than deal with face to face dialogue. These conversation topics can be applied anytime to keep things positive and upbeat. Teens need to avoid subjects that cause emotional or contentious feelings as that can lead to interpersonal conflict because of different viewpoints.

12. When speaking with or to others, name any 5 good habits to apply. (Hint: can be physical or oral habits)

 Answers will vary, but could include:
- Maintain good eye contact
- Avoid looking around room (when with an individual or small group)
- Avoid looking at a cell phone
- Stand or sit tall
- Lean forward slightly
- Don't cross arms over chest
- No fidgeting
- Acknowledge people by name
- Avoid bad language
- Clear the air when necessary (discuss areas of conflict openly rather than avoiding them)
- Remember that some things are better left unsaid
- Add to conversation by interjecting comments occasionally

- Don't randomly change the subject-transition to a new subject
- Use please, thank you, excuse me, sir and ma'am often
- Nod to show you are still listening and engaged
- Watch tone, inflection, and volume
- Avoid topics related to politics, religion, gossip, money, etc.
- Be a good listener, don't monopolize a discussion

13. Define filler word (as it pertains to oral communication).

⑨ Words (or phrases) used when someone needs time to think of what they will say next

14. Name three words or phrases (called filler words) to avoid that people typically use without realizing it?

⑨ Answers include:
- You know
- Um
- Huh
- Like
- Ah
- Hmmm
- Uhhh
- Ahhh
- Er
- OK
- Like I said…
- Right?
- Really?
- I mean…
- Well
- Yeah
- You know what I mean?
- OMG
- Awesome!

These words are often used when someone is nervous, is put on the spot, or is not sure of themselves. It happens to all of us, but if one needs time to think, just *pause in silence*. This actually gives the person or audience you are talking to time to reflect on what has already been said (which is a good thing).

Sometimes using filler words become a habit and people don't realize how often they overuse them. It takes some practice to eliminate these words from a person's speech, but it can be done.

Schools have recently increased demands for teenagers to practice their public and private speaking skills by requiring more and more assignments involving addressing both small and large groups— which is great, but may not be enough. If overuse of filler words is a concern, I suggest teens practice their speaking skills with a trusted friend or family member. Have this confidant count the number of times a favorite filler word is used and report back after a conversation. This trusted assessor can also raise his/her hand each time a filler word is used during a conversation to call to mind how often a certain word is being said. A visual reminder tends to be especially shocking, but until a person realizes the frequency of use, change cannot begin.

If a teen has to give a speech or presentation, I recommend taking a video using a smart phone and when playing it back, do a self-count (consider this is a "video-selfie"). If one employs these techniques, before you know it, problem of overusing filler words is much improved.

15. For good communication to occur, should a person listen more or speak more?

 Listen

This is where hearing and listening need to be distinguished with some teens. Hearing is letting the words enter our ears while listening is understanding and processing what truly is being said. For good communication to occur, the one speaking has to have the meaning of his/her message received in the manner it was intended. (Listening really occurs when the receiver can restate the message for clarification — I must stress that point.) Otherwise, words end up floating through the air without comprehension. I like to use the example of the teacher on the Charlie Brown cartoon. When

> *We all have two ears and one mouth, which should tell us something!*

she talks, all the students hear is, "Blah, blah, blah, blah." (Much like when I talk to my own kids sometimes! My words fall on deaf ears.) If you are not familiar with this analogy, look up an old Charlie Brown cartoon. I guarantee you a laugh!

16. **When giving a compliment, what should you always remember to do?**

 Mean it

The old saying is, "if you can't say something nice, don't say anything at all." Good advice for everyone. Compliments without genuine sincerity are worthless. Brown-nosing (i.e., giving false praise) is more transparent than adolescents realize at times.

17. **When receiving a compliment, what should you always remember?**

Accept it without denying or deflecting

Teens often will deny a compliment because they honestly don't believe it to be true (a self-esteem issue) or because they fear being viewed as conceited (whether they are or not). It is no wonder this happens. Women for centuries have deflected compliments on an outfit by saying, "This old thing!" (I have to confess I have said it too!) However, if teens assume compliments are genuine, then there is nothing wrong with simply saying, "Thank you!"

18. **When giving an apology, what should you always remember?**

 Be honest

Communication involving an apology is only good when it is sincere. Teens need to practice taking responsibility for the good and bad in their lives so it comes more naturally as adulthood approaches. During my years teaching high school, time after time I would catch students telling lies or trying to blame others for their mistakes. I made it a personal goal to convince students that "owning" an error quickly has much better results than hiding it. Plus, I'd stress that offering a solution to the problem created as a result of their mistake is not only a sign of maturity, but seems to lessen consequences (at least in many instances). After all, humans make mistakes daily, right?

Many teens find accepting an apology just as hard as giving one, so I would remind my students that a person can accept an apology without forgetting the wrong-doing.

 Demonstrating that one is a good winner or loser is often done through verbal communication. Teens need to watch what and how they say things after any form of competition.

This seemed to help many adolescents (remembering eliminates "getting burned again" by that person).

19. Explain the difference between a telephone landline and a cell phone line.

🕮 A landline is a telecommunication connection that uses a solid medium telephone line such as a metal wire or fiber optic cable laid across land (either underground or above ground from telephone pole to telephone pole)-a cell phone line uses radio waves to transmit sound through the air

A landline (also called a fixed-line or wire line) uses metal wire to transmit sound through a house or building's telephone wiring to connect to the public system available in a local area. This is why a landline is considered "hard-wired" and not mobile. This phone system has good quality with fewer occurrences of dropped calls and requires no charging. A landline number is listed in a telephone directory and has precise 911 tracking in case of emergency.

In contrast to a landline, a cellular phone works like a two-way radio or walkie-talkie. A transmitter converts a voice into an electrical signal via radio waves. The nearest cell tower receives the message and passes it to the next cell tower. These relayed radio waves reach the person being called after being converted back to voice sounds. Currently, cell phone numbers are not listed in a telephone directory, but their use is transportable — a real plus.

Understanding the basic differences allow teens to appreciate and use both types of communication. However, as technology improves, the advantages of a landline are rapidly being applied to cellular phones and will cause teens to question whether having a landline in their home is worthwhile.

20. When placing a long distance call from a landline in the U.S., what does a person need to dial before the ten-digit telephone number? Why?

> **(?)** Dial a "1" first to indicate the number is not local and going to another area because a call won't go through without it in many cases

In the past, using the "1" also indicated the call being placed was long-distance and would incur an additional charge. With the abundance of telephone services offered today, this isn't necessarily the case anymore. However, a landline still requires the "1" to be dialed before the ten-digit phone number for "direction," if you will. This "1" is called a *country code*. Additionally, teens should know that every country has its own *country code*. For example, Germany has the country code of "49," Japan is "81," and Italy is "39."[8]

To place an international call, a person will need to use an *international prefix number first* (the number needed to connect *out* of the country you are currently *in*)...followed by a country code, a city code (area code) and phone number (a varying number of digits depending on the country the call is going to). "011" is the international prefix number to call out of the United States. So, if a caller in the U.S. wanted to call the Dunedin City Council, in New Zealand, he/she would dial 011 64 3 477 4000.[9] ("64" is New Zealand's country code and the other numbers direct the call to the council specifically.)

---

8 http://www.howtocallabroad.com/codes.html
9 http://www.dunedin.govt.nz/

Teenagers need to keep in mind that in other countries, the number of total digits needed to be dialed can be different than the 1 + 10 digits we are accustomed to in the U.S. For example, to call Tokyo, Japan, you would use the "011" (international prefix code) + "81" (country code), "3" (city code) and then phone number which is 8 digits in length. Check the internet for specific instructions and international and country codes when needed.

One last thing, don't think a phone number written with + signs between digits (i.e., 011 + 61 + xxx + xxxx) requires the use of a plus sign throughout. *You do not enter these plus signs.* A plus sign can only be used as a short cut for an international exit code when using a cell phone. (With advanced technology on a cell phone, you can literally enter a plus sign before the number—found by holding the "0" key. Cell phone devices allow this and will automatically know you are dialing an international call and the international exit code numbers can be omitted.)

Jen, an Advanced Marketing and college prep student of mine, was given the assignment of ordering pens with our high school logo printed on them. As a class, I had reviewed what information to provide when ordering a product by telephone and some tips on telephone etiquette. I then gave Jen the long distance number and sent her to place the order using the school phone on my office desk. A minute later, she walked out of my office and announced to the class, "That company is out of business!"

I turned and said, "They can't be. I just called and ordered from them last week. What makes you say that?"

Jen proceeded to explain that when she dialed the telephone number there was a message that said, "Call cannot be completed as dialed." I chuckled, but the other teens in the room didn't see the humor or error.

"Jen, did you dial a 1 before the number I gave you?" I asked.

"No! Why?"

Right then, I stopped class and gave a short lecture to everyone on the difference between a landline and cell phone and how their use would be different if dialing outside our town and the local area code. Faces around the room displayed shock, followed by enlightenment.

21. When calling a place of business, what are the first three pieces of information you should supply when someone answers?

   Your name, who you would like to speak to, purpose of the call

It is no secret that teenagers prefer communicating by text and email. However, there are times when verbal communication must occur to someone other than a friend (e.g., job opportunity, customer service issue, college admission office, etc.), hence the need for this knowledge and some practice. When making a business call, young people need to know to treat the call as if it were a meeting. Have an agenda, get to the point, and be brief so everyone can move on with his/her day. If the call is of a personal nature and one is calling to "chat," it is still courteous to make sure everyone has enough time for that.

On both professional and personal calls, watch background noises like paper shuffling, music or TV sounds, and computer keystrokes. I stress not talking on the phone with food, gum, or candy in your mouth as receivers can amplify these sounds. Also, cover the receiver if there is a need to cough or sneeze (mute buttons are great tools for this).

If you have a scheduled call, be at your desk or in a quiet place on time to receive that call.

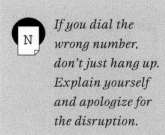

22. When leaving a telephone message, what information should be included?

Your name, phone number you want used when returning the call, purpose of the call

If you dial the wrong number, don't just hang up. Explain yourself and apologize for the disruption.

Regardless of whether a message is being left on an answering machine or dictated to a person, the information to be given is the same. It should be spoken slowly and clearly and even repeated, if time permits.

Barney had been admiring Madge from afar for weeks. He finally got up enough nerve to call her, but no one answered. He said, "Madge, this is Barney. Sorry I missed you. Please call me back."

When Madge heard the message, she was thrilled until she realized she didn't have his number to call him back. Barney assumed she could or would use caller ID. Big mistake!

23. What is the proper way to answer a home telephone?

Answers may vary, but any of the following are acceptable:

- "Hello."
- "Hello, Smith (i.e., family name) residence."
- "Hello, Karen (i.e., your name) speaking."

Teens need to be pleasant, clear, and avoid casual greetings like "Whuz-up?" or "Yo!" when answering any phone. One never knows who is on the other end, so showing maturity by staying

With today's technology, teens need to know how call forwarding works.

*Dialing *69 after a call will display the previous telephone number for call back.*

*Dialing *67 after placing a call will prevent a call recipient from using the *69 function.*

focused on the caller and his/her needs is important. Another stellar practice when answering the telephone is to remember not to alert a person at the other end of the house that a phone call is for them by screaming their name without muting the phone (you laugh, but you know exactly what I am talking about).

I would be remiss to not mention here that teens may need a reminder that no matter their age, they should never reveal to a caller that they are home alone. Also, the reason someone cannot come to the phone is not to be disclosed, especially if something private is happening (e.g., bathroom usage, fighting with a family member, etc.). Never give personal information like credit card numbers, social security numbers, or financial information over the phone unless you initiated the call and are confident in who you are sharing information with.

24. When taking a telephone message for someone else, what information should be included?

Name of person calling, company if applicable, purpose of call or message, call back telephone number, date, and time of call-additionally, you can ask when is a good time for the recipient to return the call

After taking a message, teens need to know that repeating all the information given by a caller before hanging up is as important as displaying the message prominently to ensure the receiver sees it. Additionally, there may be a slightly different message protocol requirement in a place of business, so one should find out from a co-worker the company expectations.

25. What is the acceptable length of time to put someone on hold?

 Max of one minute

The acceptable amount of time is not etched in stone, but respecting someone's time is. If you think about it, it shouldn't take more than 20-30 seconds to answer another call and offer to call that person back. If a second call comes in and it is not an emergency, optimally a person would just ignore the new call. However, preparing a caller in advance that you may have to cut their call short due to an urgent call coming in, is permissable.

<u>Misc. Vocab</u> - Define the following oral communication related terms...

26. Three-way Calling/Conferencing

 Adding a third person to a telephone conversation

A three-way call is generated by one person (Caller A). Here are the steps:[10]

→ Caller A dials another individual (Caller B) and tells them about the third person to be added.

→ Caller A will quickly press and release the call/talk (cell phone) or flash (landline phone) button.

→ When Caller A hears a dial tone, he/she dials Caller C's number.

→ When Caller C answers, Caller A presses the call/talk or flash button again and everyone should be connected.

Caller A can add up to five people max. Also, the call originator (Caller A) should *research the exact steps to be taken based on the type of phone they are using.* The above instructions are general in nature and may differ with different phones. Caller A will also need to make sure their phone has the three-way calling features and know if long distance and airtime charges apply. The originator is the only one who can end a call completely, but Caller B and C can get off the line any time they see fit.

If more than five participants are involved, this is then called "conference calling" (although this total number can vary). There are services that will set-up a conference call for you and provide a phone number to each caller to "dial in" and be connected. Make sure you identify yourself when you are connected so everyone knows exactly who is on the call and who may be missing. Conference calling is used most commonly in a business setting, not in a home environment.

---

10 http://www.wikihow.com/Make-a-Three-Way-Phone-Call

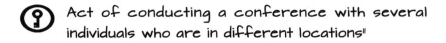

27. Teleconferencing

> Act of conducting a conference with several individuals who are in different locations[11]

Telephones, computers, televisions (video), internet, and radio are some of the tools that are utilized to successfully carry out a teleconference. Connecting participants in different locations via telecommunication equipment for the purpose of having a meeting or group discussion with the ability to see and hear all participants is videoconferencing.

28. How many feet should be between someone using a cell phone and another individual?

> Ten feet, in all directions

Ten feet would ensure that no one is infringed upon by cell phone use. Keep in mind a reasonable volume level must be maintained and very personal discussions should not take place in public areas no matter the distance from others.

29. List five or more places where it is inappropriate to use your cell phone.

> Answers will vary, but could include:
> - Bathrooms (especially public)
> - Elevators
> - Hospitals

---

11 https://www.eztalks.com/resource/main-difference-between-tele-conferencing-and-video-conferencing.html

- Places
  of worship
- Office
  waiting rooms
- Auditoriums
- Schools
- Restaurants
- Dining table
- Meetings
- Libraries
- Museums
- Taxis/Buses/Trains/Planes (any public transport in proximity to other commuters)
- Anytime you are in the presence of another person

- Live theater
  performances
- Funerals
- Weddings
- Movie theaters
- Check-out lines
- Church
- Driving (also as a passenger)
- Walking

When was the last time you saw a teenager (or an adult for that matter) without a cell phone in his/her ear or hand? Hmmmm…long time, huh? Yep, cell phones are a necessary tool in life these days. No one can dispute that cell phones have many uses and are convenient, but they can be a source of contention. My point is that *cell phones don't have to be an issue if everyone* (because this isn't just a teenager problem) *would observe some basic rules of etiquette* when it comes to these electronic devices. *The short of it is to be respectful of those around you!*

I went out to dinner with my family last summer to a casual, local establishment. We were busy sharing with each other the events of our day when I stopped everyone and asked them to look at the family of five to the right. As all eyes turned in that direction, I continued with "I can't believe four of the five individuals at that table are on their cell phones and ignoring each other. What is the point of going out to dinner together if they'd rather be talking and interacting with someone else?"

My daughter chimed in, "And look at that poor little boy. He must only be about six. He is climbing all over everyone, is under the table, playing with the drapes, bored stiff, and all because no one is paying attention to him. Mom, you would have never put up with me behaving like that in a restaurant at that age!"

We laughed at Leah's recall, but it saddened us at the same time. I wonder how many others in the restaurant took notice of this family's etiquette and found it unfortunate ... or were they also on their phones and never noticed?

Guidelines for general cell phone use:

- Use the *ten-foot rule*. This means a person should stay a minimum of ten feet away from another person when talking on a cell phone (in all directions) — find a private place to talk.
- Avoid cell phone use when you are face to face with anyone (this includes texting). It gives the impression to another individual that they aren't important enough to receive your full attention.
- Talk softly and don't use the speaker. (You *are not* so interesting and others really do not want to hear you.)
- Remove both ear buds to show respect if someone approaches you.
- No humming, singing, or laughing loudly while using a cell phone.
- If asked to turn the cell phone off, do it (often the case in group gatherings).
- Never talk about personal issues in public where others could overhear.

- No multi-tasking — if you need to use the phone, make that a solo activity.
- Always turn off your phone during a group meal and don't set it on the table.
- If an important call is expected, announce ahead of time and excuse yourself to take it.
- Choose ring tones and volume settings wisely. Blow horns, dog whistle, screams, etc. would be examples of possible offensive ring tones. The volume needs to be set so you can hear it when it is close — not loud enough to hear across the room.
- Changing the setting to vibrate often isn't enough — the phone needs to be off during a movie, interview, meal, etc. Vibrations can be felt and phones light up which is annoying to others.
- Don't send embarrassing pictures to others via a cell phone.
- Don't put someone on speakerphone without alerting them.

I hadn't seen Denise and Christine for years and while traveling to Jacksonville, FL we arranged to have lunch together. Christine had her two teenage children, Morgan & Tristan, with her so we asked for a table for seven and started chatting immediately.

After three hours of much laughter, storytelling, and catching up, we paid the bill and started to leave the table.

"Gosh Christine. You have done a wonderful job raising these two kids. They put up with all our gabbing today and I didn't even see them try to peek at their cell phones one time!" I exclaimed.

Morgan and Tristan broke out into full laughter immediately.

"What's so funny?" I inquired.

"Well, my mom has a thing about cell phones during a meal and we get in big trouble if we even think about using them at the table," Morgan replied.

"Yep! She is really mean about it too!" Tristan added as Christine shook her head in agreement.

Now we all started to chuckle as my husband said, "Well I am impressed. Your mom is teaching you both the right thing and others will notice. You both will go far in life if you continue to do as your mom tells you. It is very impressive and I for one will not soon forget meeting you both."

 Additional guidelines for cell phone texting can be found in the next chapter under Written Correspondence.

Since oral communication is about making others know that they are important and that you are delighted to be in contact with them, teens must adopt the attitude of doing the right thing by *always talking like a lady (or gentleman) when communicating* (whether in person or over the phone). These practices when communicating orally set the tone for future encounters.

The landline...LET IT GO! The youth of our society may not be able to afford two phone systems and are connected so strongly to their cell phones that it is like another appendage. This isn't going to change, so just equip them with the correct etiquette to use their cell.

⑦ Written Correspondence

1. What is meant by the term "legal signature"?

2. Write out your legal signature 5 times.

3. How far in advance should an invitation be sent for the following?
   - a. a wedding
   - b. a party
   - c. a business meeting

4. When should a thank you note be sent after receiving a gift or gesture of kindness?

5. Should thank you notes be handwritten, typed, sent via email, or via text message?

6. List 3 rules related to writing thank you notes.

7. Name 3 reasons a person would want to write a letter.

8. When using a computer to type a non-personal letter, what is the standard font size to use?

9. When using a computer to type a non-personal letter, what should you remember concerning which font style to use?

10. When writing a non-personal letter, name the different parts of the letter to be included.

11. If Beth Ann Carey wrote a letter and Rachel Marie Sams typed it, what would the end notation line look like?

12. When a sender includes additional paper(s) in an envelope with a letter, what are these papers called in an end notation?

13. When someone else will be receiving and viewing the same hard copy letter, how is that indicated in an end notation?

14. If a letter is sent via email, how do you indicate a copy is being sent to another person?

15. Type (or handwrite) a business letter to a company explaining your disappointment with a faulty product. Use proper letter format (block style, modified block style, or modified semi-block style) with all the expected letter parts and punctuation.

16. List the names of all fifty states in the U.S. with the corresponding two-letter abbreviation for each state. (No using a resource other than your brain!)

17. Address an envelope to your best friend's parent(s). Must include appropriate spacing, a return address, two letter state abbreviations, and a drawn on stamp in the proper location.

18. Memo is derived from what Latin word?

19. When and where would you find a memo being used?

20. List the required headings used on a memorandum.

 21. Write a memo announcing to the family that you have just won a trip to Disneyland and they are all invited to go. Must be in correct memo format and include all headings with proper punctuation.

<u>Misc. Vocab</u>-Define the following written correspondence related words...

22. Downloading
23. Installing
24. Copying
25. Sexting

26. What is your email address? Is it appropriate to use throughout adulthood?

27. List 5 rules of social decorum related to being "online" (i.e., netiquette)

28. List 5 rules of social decorum related to "texting" (i.e., textiquette).

⑨ Written Correspondence

Written correspondence — a social skill involving putting words onto paper to communicate with others. Is that right? Should I say a social skill involving putting words into a computer, phone, or tablet to communicate? Does it even matter which vehicle is used to correspond with others? Is there more to this chapter than just letter and note writing? Yes, there is!

TC Teenagers have had little need to correspond in writing in life so far, and when they do, they have used electronic forms of communication (for the most part). Even passing notes in class has been replaced with texting a message. On that point, no debate is needed. The reality in today's world is that professors in college (and teachers in high school) have students submitting papers online and many textbooks have online versions now. (Are you perhaps reading this book electronically?) The majority of new hires are issued laptops and smart phones on the first day and are expected to use both efficiently. So, the fact that many students today cannot read cursive writing and even less are able to write in cursive isn't surprising. Cursive is no longer taught in elementary school in most states. Grades for penmanship disappeared decades ago and the debate as to whether this is a travesty or not will probably continue for years to come. Truthfully, there is an uncertainty about how written communication will be done in the future. However currently, teens need to be proficient with handwritten *and* electronic correspondence and apply the etiquette guidelines to both.

The good news is that the majority of guidelines that revolve around writing are the same for electronic and handwritten connections. Teens will be able to choose their preferred vehicle once they learn the rules and I hope they gain perspective from this chapter. Knowing and following the expectations in regards to written correspondence will make a teen stand out, in a good way, and that is always the goal!

Here's What A Teen Needs To Know ...

I. What is meant by the term "legal signature"?

An authentic, unique mark, sign, or name that is hand written on a document to signify knowledge, approval, and obligation-must be in cursive and look the same each time it is written

Some teenagers may not be familiar with this term. Sure, they write their name all the time, but often do it differently depending on their mood. Everyone needs to know how to write *(in cursive)* the name printed on their birth certificate to qualify as their legal signature. Nicknames, even shortened given name (e.g., Ben is short for Benjamin), cannot be used on documents requiring a *legal signature* (although I'm not sure how closely this is monitored). Consistency is most important and applies to documents like driver's license, passport, contracts, financial papers, etc.

All of this is important to reduce the risk of identity theft, impersonation, and fraud (a real threat these days). Handwriting comparison/analysis can easily demonstrate you are who you say you are. If a person's signature looks different each time it is written, this can't be accomplished. I recommend teenagers create a legal signature now and start using it (practice makes perfect, as they say). And I would consider using the middle name initial as part of this signature. After all, there are many individuals with the name John Smith, but not as many who were born as John Z. Smith (for John Zachary Smith).

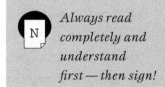

Always read completely and understand first — then sign!

Lynn was so excited about her trip to Russia, as her only son was marrying a wonderful Russian girl in late September. She and her husband had been to Mexico and the Bahamas before, but this was their first trip to the other side of the world. They researched and made lists to ensure nothing would be forgotten or overlooked. They gathered all needed paperwork and packed with anticipation. Everything seemed to be going smoothly for the big event.

Lynn and Jerry arrived at the airport two hours before their flight departed and went directly to the airline desk. Unfortunately, the check-in desk was as far as Lynn's trip took her. With tears streaming, she waved goodbye to her husband as he went through security.

You see, there was inconsistency in how Lynn's name appeared on her passport, license, and airline ticket (a discrepancy in her printed "legal" names and signatures on the different documents). The airline personnel would not let her continue her journey because of this. Her only wedding memories are those that came in a stack of 4" x 6" photos.

 2. Write out your legal signature 5 times.

Names obviously will vary, but signatures must be in cursive and look the same

The goal is to develop a *legible* signature (if it isn't already too late). However, as long as a signature is written the same way every time, it will suffice regardless of legibility. We have all seen scribble and lines used instead of letters and it passes every time because it is the same every time!

3. How far in advance should an invitation be sent for the following?

   a. A wedding

   6 to 8 weeks

   b. A party

   2 to 3 weeks

   c. A business meeting

   Depends, but as much time as possible

Since weddings are typically a once in a lifetime affair that you don't want anyone to miss, sending the invitation out with adequate notice is crucial. "Save the Date" cards or magnets announcing this important date months in advance has allowed an invitee to mark their calendar, but the date in which an invitation should be mailed has not changed.

When it comes to parties, a couple of weeks is typically enough time to get a good crowd for a party. (If not inviting electronically, allow for "snail mail" delays.) Business meeting invites are not as easy to state a mailing date for because there are many factors to consider. Is travel involved? How many people will be coming to the event? How crucial is the topic? What length of time was used in the past? What is the relationship with this person or group? The best advice I can give teenagers is to allow as much time as possible, be flexible, and allow for accommodations in setting business meetings.

Here are some other suggested timelines that can help to guide:[12]

Event	When To Invite
Anniversary party	3–6 weeks
Bar or Bat Mitzvah	1 month
Bon Voyage party	Last minute–3 weeks
Casual party	Same day–2 weeks
Charity Ball	6 weeks–3 months
Christmas party	1 month
Cocktail party	1–4 weeks
Debutante Ball	6 weeks–3 months
Formal dinner	3–6 weeks
Graduation party	3 weeks
Holiday dinner	2 weeks–2 months
Housewarming party	Few days–3 weeks
Informal dinner	Few days–3 weeks
Lunch or Tea	Few days–2 weeks

One should not extend an invitation to another person without getting permission from the original host/hostess. This includes social media invites.

---

12 http://emilypost.com/advice/invitation-timing/

4. When should a thank you note be sent after receiving a gift or gesture of kindness?

 As soon as possible

 Due to the number of thank you notes involved with wedding gifts, the timeline is extended to 6 weeks with a max of 3 months.

I like teens to get into the habit of sending a thank you note *immediately* upon receiving a gift when a giver is not present to thank in person. This practice ensures one does not forget and makes a quick and powerful impression. If the immediate action intent fails, shoot for two weeks and certainly within the month.

Often my students would say, "Mrs. Carey, what types of things call for a thank you note?" I would let them know that a person can never go wrong sending a thank you note for anything, but definitely after the following:

1. Receiving gifts (birthday, baby, wedding, housewarming, congratulatory, etc.)
2. Attending dining events
3. Getting condolence notes and gifts
4. After job interviews
5. When gifts are received during illness

Teens may think one sends a thank you note only to ensure future presents will be given or additional invitations will come their way (a valid point, actually). However, hopefully teenagers also know that the best reason to send thank you notes *is to demonstrate common*

 Graduation announcements do not mandate a gift.

courtesy. Even if a gift isn't something you are fond of, being grateful for the thought is important (just do not say anything about not liking it).

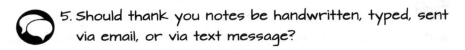

Who doesn't love their birthday? Good wishes, cake, parties and presents!! Year after year my friend, Debbie, mailed all her nieces and nephews living out of town gifts on their birthday. They got toys when they were little, cool clothes, and gift cards/money as they grew. Gifts went to the kids year after year, but never a thank you note was sent. No phone call of appreciation. No email either. Unless she sent a check, which had to be cashed, Debbie never knew if anyone received their gift. Debbie got fed up! She stopped sending gifts to these members of her family.

5. Should thank you notes be handwritten, typed, sent via email, or via text message?

⑨ Hand written notes are the best

Notes written by hand demonstrate extra effort and a personal touch, so that is the best approach. However, if a person's handwriting is atrocious (preventing the receiver from reading it easily), then using a computer is advised. Using the computer to print a thank you letter or sending an email (or text) thank you is obviously better than sending nothing. Emails and text messages should only be utilized if time is of the essence (which shouldn't be the case unless procrastination is happening-LOL) or when a mailing address isn't attainable. Always use blue or black ink and nice stationery or a note card.

Remembering that a thank you note is going to make someone else feel appreciated and special will help teens develop this habit. Sure, it makes the sender look good, but that shouldn't be the primary reason for writing it and if teens keep that in mind, the writing seems to come more easily.

Don't start off with the trite "Thank you for ... " Engage in a conversation related to news in your current life or relive part of the event that catapulted the need for this note (it's like "small talk" in writing). Then, one should say how much you appreciate the gift, gesture, hospitality, whatever! Spell out exactly what you are thankful for — the gift by name, the recommendation letter, the dinner party, the accommodations, etc. If you received money as a gift, there is no need to mention the amount, but do mention how you plan to spend that money (hopefully spending in a responsible way).

Steve and Jessie graduated college and had a wonderful wedding celebration that my husband and I attended. Two weeks after the wedding, we received a thank you note for our gift. It read, "Thank you so much for sharing our special day. We really like the hand-crafted vase and will think of you when we use it. Steve and Jessie"

I was impressed to have a thank you so quickly, but was surprised that there was no mention of what they intended to do with the check that we also included. I checked my bank statement and the check hadn't cleared, so I waited. A month later, the check still hadn't been cashed so I reached out to Steve to inquire. He couldn't remember for sure seeing the check and told me he would check with Jessie and get back to me.

Sure enough, he found the check with the cards and was very apologetic. I told him that I thought it was odd that the thank you had no mention of using the check for a new house item as they were specific in their mention of the other gift.

We both laughed a little and he told me, "You know my mom raised me right!"

6. List 3 rules related to writing thank you notes.

 Answers will vary, but could include:
- Always send when giver is not available in person to thank
- Handwrite if possible
- Use good handwriting and grammar
- Use blue or black ink
- Sending an email or text is better than no thank you
- Use personalized stationary if possible
- Send promptly
- Specify item or gesture you are thankful for
- Discuss use of gift
- Use heartfelt sentiment
- Always use a salutation (greeting) with recipient's name
- Use appropriate closing and sign

Personal thank you notes use a greeting and closing followed by a comma. Dear _____, is standard and closings vary depending on the relationship the recipient has with the giver. Options would include: Love, Yours Truly, With Love, Sincerely, Regards, With Gratitude, With Appreciation, etc.

7. Name 3 reasons a person would want to write a letter.

 Answers will vary, but could include:
- To communicate information
- To have a record of a correspondence and eliminate oral discrepancies

- Personal way to stay in touch
- To surprise or please others
- To demonstrate good etiquette
- To impress someone with writing skills
- To receive letters in return
- To have fun and engage in a creative endeavor

8. When using a computer to type a non-personal letter, what is the standard font size to use?

🔑 **Size 10-12 point** (11 is typically the default)

Font size is a personal preference when it comes to writing personal correspondence. However, for business or formal writing, a writer will need to adjust the font size based on the length of the letter and try to keep the correspondence to one page.

9. When using a computer to type a non-personal letter, what should you remember concerning which font style to use?

🔑 Consider your audience and choose a professional looking font that is easy to read

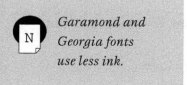

Garamond and Georgia fonts use less ink.

The most common font styles are Times New Roman, **Verdana**, or Arial (Arial or Helvetica on a Mac), but using other fonts will work as long as they are legible and fit the occasion.

10. When writing a non-personal letter, name the different parts of the letter to be included.

- Sender's Address OR Company Logo Letterhead (if applicable)
- Today's Date
- Inside Address (recipient's name and address)
- Greeting or Salutation (the beginning of the letter)
- Body (message of the letter)
- Closing (polite ending of the letter)
- Signature
- End Notations (used only if applicable and include initials of typist, enclosures, and cc/c/Copy to)

When writing a personal letter to a friend or family member, there are no guidelines on how to set-up the correspondence. However, if a letter is of a professional or formal nature, the writer needs to use the expected layout and include all the parts listed above with proper punctuation and line spacing.

 Alignment, justification, spacing, and general set-up of these letter parts will be illustrated in subsequent pages.

Here is an overview of letter parts:

- **SENDER'S ADDRESS** – A letter starts with the street address of the sender (not a name), followed by the city, state, and zip code on the next line. The current date is placed on the following line. If writing a letter as a business representative, company letterhead is often used. When this occurs, the current date would be the first line of typed information.

Letterhead is special stationery with a heading that includes a company name, address (i.e., sender's address), and company logo (a unique representation or symbol) at the top of the page (or combination top and bottom). It may include the company telephone number, website, and even an email address. Using letterhead allows the letter writer to skip typing an address as it is already provided.

- **RECIPIENT'S ADDRESS** – This *inside address* includes the name of the person you are writing, his/her title, company name, and full address (occupying 3–5 lines).
- **GREETING** – The greeting or salutation comes next. It commonly starts with the word *Dear* and is followed by the recipient's title or name. The punctuation is always a colon (:) in a professional letter (e.g., Dear Ms. Abercrombie: or Dear Personnel Director:) and a comma (,) in personal writing (e.g., Dear Aunt Peggy,).
- **LETTER BODY** – Every letter has text, which is written in paragraphs, and is called the "body" of a letter. The writer's message or content is to be given here and varies in length.
- **CLOSING** – The closing culminates or ends the letter and is followed by a comma (,) in both professional and personal letters.
- **SIGNATURE** – This letter part is often referred to as the *signature block*. It requires the writer's handwritten signature, in cursive with blue or black ink (so leave 4–5 blank lines to ensure enough space). The writer's name, followed by their title (if applicable) is then typed.
- **END NOTATIONS** – End notations may be needed if someone other than the writer does the typing of the letter, enclosures

(additional papers) are provided with the letter, or copies of the letter are sent to more than one person. End notes are placed below the signature block and *are only used if they apply.* Each end notation is placed on its own line and the order in which these notations are provided varies with different sources and preferences.

II. **If Beth Ann Carey wrote a letter and Rachel Marie Sams typed it, what would the end notation line look like?**

  BAC/rms

Someday when a teen is an adult, they may be fortunate enough to have an assistant on the job to help type and process a letter. When a *person types a correspondence for another person*, this is noted in the letter after the signature block.

Here are the guidelines to follow:

- The reference initials appear two lines below the last line of the signature block
- The writer's initials are included in all CAPS, followed by a forward slash mark
- The typist's initials are then placed in lower case letters
- Example: BAC/rms (indicating I wrote and signed the letter, but my assistant Rachel Marie Sams typed it)

It "looks" more personal if a letter comes from a person, so companies often use ghostwriters. In this case, no credit is given in an end notation and you will not know who actually wrote or typed the letter.

If the *writer of a letter is different from the person signing and sending the letter*, this is also noted in after the signature block.

The guidelines go like this:

- The signer's initials appear first in CAPS, followed by a forward slash mark
- The writer's initials appear next in CAPS, followed by a forward slash mark
- The typist's appear last in lower case
- Example: JLJ/BAC/rms (indicating I wrote the letter, Rachel typed it, and Janet Louise Joswiak initiated and therefore is sending and signing the letter)

Enclosures are called "attachments" in an email.

However, the most common scenario is when a letter writer is the *sender and typist* (explaining the decline in personal assistants/secretaries and increased use of computers by everyone). In this case, no end notation is needed because the signature block indicates who wrote and typed the letter.

12. When a sender includes additional paper(s) in an envelope with a letter, what are these papers called in an end notation?

 Enclosure or Enclosures

Enclosure simply makes the recipient aware that there is additional paper (or papers — Enclosures) provided beyond the letter itself.

Here are the guidelines for this end notation:

- Typed beneath any typist's initials (if there are any)
- Starts with a capital "E"
- If multiple enclosures are included, the number of enclosed documents will appear directly after, in parentheses
- Example: Enclosure or Enclosures (3)

> N *No punctuation is used with end notations.*

13. When someone else will be receiving and viewing the same hard copy letter, how is that indicated in an end notation?

> Use cc: followed by the name(s) of anyone receiving a copy

Email has not completely replaced the need for hard copy letters (especially in the business realm) today. To ensure teens understand protocol for both processes, they need to know that cc: is used.

> N *c: is acceptable, however it can be confused with PC drive letters so you might want to avoid it.*

Historically, cc: stood for *carbon copies* because carbon paper (or tissue) was used to transfer or make copies of a letter. Today it often refers to *courtesy copy* as carbon paper has been replaced with copy machines and computer printers. Copy to: (note the C is capitalized) or c: (for copy) are two other options.

Here are the tips for using all versions:

- Lower case (exception is Copy to:)
- Followed by a colon and a space
- A listing of names to receive a copy follows
- Example: cc: John Smith

If multiple people are getting a copy, then it is common to list the names in alphabetical order or by hierarchy, underneath each other. (Don't hesitate to put a comma after the name and add the person's job title.) If there are several recipients, skip two spaces after the colon and align each name in a vertical list. Here are examples of how each would look:

cc: Billy Bob
       Mary Canary
       John Smith

c: Billy Bob
    Mary Canary
    John Smith

Copies to: Billy Bob, VP
            John Smith, HR Manager
            Mary Canary, Accounting Clerk

This would be one of those times where an older adult may want to take time and explain life before copy machines, printers, and scanners. Most teens have never heard of carbon paper, yet alone seen it. It's fun to see if they can grasp a paper-like product, coated with dark waxy pigment containing carbon, which would transfer writing or typing onto another piece of paper placed beneath the original paper. This underneath second copy (or copies) could then be sent to others without having to write a duplicate over and over. (Don't forget details of how the carbon would get all over your hands and smudged easily, causing a writer to have to start over!) And if any readers are old enough to recall the blue worksheets in school that were created from ditto machines, go ahead and explain some of that old technology. Descriptions of that machine (and how dittos smelled) will really have teens howling at how barbaric things were in "the olden days" (and demonstrate again how good they have it).

14. If a letter is sent via email, how do you indicate a copy is being sent to another person?

🧿 Use CC: line in the email header or use ec: (electronic copy) as an end notation in place of cc: on actual letter

Another abbreviation that teens should get familiar with is BCC: — Blind Carbon Copy (and they probably are). This notation is found in an email header and allows an individual to send the same message to multiple people. A writer would use this to prevent recipients from knowing how many different people got the same message and keeps email addresses anonymous. Using this tool eliminates the deplorable habit of clicking the "Reply All" button by someone when they really should only be replying to the original sender (just sayin').

L.I.F.E.

 15. Type (or handwrite) a business letter to a company explaining your disappointment with a faulty product. Use proper letter format (block style, modified block style, or modified semi-block style) with all the expected letter parts, spacing, and punctuation.

> Letters will vary—for full credit, letters should match one of the sample letter formats to follow and include all letter parts with correct spacing, indentations, punctuations, and margins (look for partial credit too)

Yes, a person can use the internet, Microsoft Word, Google Docs, etc. for hundreds of template choices. However, I recommend teenagers master one these three sample formats now and their woes will be over throughout adulthood (except for creating a solid message, of course).

Here are the generic guidelines that apply to all three letter styles:

- Margins are set at 1–1.5 inches.
- Single spaced.
- A comma comes after the city, followed by a space, and the 2-letter state abbreviation.
- Put 2 spaces after the state abbreviation and then the zip code.
- The body of the letter (sometimes called the copy or text of a correspondence) can have as many paragraphs as needed to convey a message. However, most formal correspondence is kept to one page.

- Use of good grammar, punctuation, sentence structure, and spell check is expected.
- There are 3 blank lines between the date and the inside address with a single blank line used between all other parts of the letter (including the start of a new paragraph).
- If a letter is extremely short in length, the typist can eye-ball the vertical centering and make an adjustment. (Place the cursor at the start of the first line of text and use the enter button to shift the entire letter down the page a few lines. A writer can also customize the margin settings.) This centering will make the letter visually more appealing on the page and not appear "top heavy" (think of typed words as having weight — avoid being top heavy on the page).
- Consider your audience and choose font style (and size) so a reader is encouraged to read it.
- A colon (:) always follows the greeting/salutation in business correspondence.
- A comma (,) follows an informal, personal greeting/salutation (e.g., writing to a Grandfather or friend).
- A comma (,) follows the closing in both business and personal letters.

Do not use "Thank You" as a closing, as that should be part of the body of a letter.

The use of "open punctuation" is an alternative in letter writing whereby the colon and commas after the salutation and closing are omitted.

Handwritten letters follow the same format as a typed letter.

- The most widely used closing is Sincerely, but other common closings include Regards, Best, Best Wishes, Yours Truly, Cordially, With Warm Regard, or Respectfully.
- After the closing, 4–5 lines are left blank (to provide space for hand signing the letter) — the sender's name (and title, if applicable) are then typed or printed as many signatures are not legible.
- After printing a letter, the sender should use blue or black ink to sign their name in cursive. (If sending a letter electronically, no signature is required. Just type sender's name in plain text.)

I wouldn't be surprised if some teens balk at the idea of writing a professional (or personal) letter at their age (my children did). However, I promise there will be an occasion when they will *need* to write a letter for something. Since letters are often written and attached (or copied) to an email as well, teens might as well learn the layout now and be ready.

Companies tend to favor one letter format over another, so one should ask before writing a letter on-the-job.

Recognizing different letter styles can also help when reading correspondence. I suggest teens review some letters received in the mail with an adult and discuss how the overall appearance impacts getting the message across to the recipient. Letter formats give messages a certain feel or tone that impact meaning and understanding.

Handwritten letters follow the same line spacing and information layout as the typed samples in this chapter.

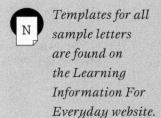

A sample *BLOCK LETTER* layout appears on the next page. This letter style is the most likely letter format to resemble a teen's correspondence as it is taught by the majority of middle and high school teachers today. It is the easiest style to remember because all lines are left justified and a writer needs only to learn and memorize the spacing (simple as that). However, teens are free to pick the format they like best (a great example of empowerment).

Templates for all sample letters are found on the Learning Information For Everyday website.

Here is the tip that is unique to a block style letter:

- No indenting when using the straight block style.

In all 3 sample letters, the information to be provided on each line is indicated in parentheses and italics. The numbers in parentheses at the end of each line or paragraph indicate the number of times the typist should hit the "enter" button at that point. This will ensure the correct line spacing in the letter (e.g., (2X) means you hit enter two times, leaving one blank line and start to type again on the following line). These are given as a learning tool and are not to be typed in a letter. (Margin pre-sets or the use of styles can also facilitate this process.)

BLOCK FORMAT SAMPLE

100 Anywhere Street *(sender's street address)*
Atlanta, GA 30301 *(sender's city, state & zip code)*
May 1, 20__ *(current date) (4X)*

Mr. Jeremy Williams, Customer Service Mgr. *(recipient's name & applicable title)*
Retail USA *(company name)*
16 W 36th Street *(recipient's street address)*
New York, NY 10018 *(recipient's city, state & zip code) (2X)*

Dear Mr. Williams: *(greeting/salutation, followed with a colon) (2X)*

I recently bought two pairs of your "Tiny Tummy 101" jeans for my daughter. She was pleased with the fit and construction when I bought them, but not after the first washing. One pair came out of the wash looking like it is five years old and ready for the rag barrel. *(2X)*

So you know, both pairs of jeans were washed together according to the label instructions. The one pair lost half of the sequins on the back pocket, the seams are fraying, and the left hem is coming out. These are $70 jeans and we expected them to last more than one wash cycle!

I contacted the store where I purchased them and they told me to contact you. I have enclosed a copy of the receipt and am requesting a full refund for both pairs as I have lost confidence in your product. Please send the refund to the address at the top of this letter. I will await instructions on what you want me to do with the jeans going forward.

Sincerely, *(4-5X)*

Beth Carey *(cursive signature in blue or black ink on hard copies only)*
Beth Carey *(typed name of sender)*
Mother *(2X) (typed title of sender)*

BAC/rms *(writer's initials/typist's initials)*
Enclosure *(shows additional paper is enclosed)*
cc: Leah Carey *(name of individual who is getting a copy of this letter)*

A sample *MODIFIED BLOCK* LETTER layout appears on the next page. All the tips for using this style mimic block style with one exception.

Here is the tip that is unique to a modified block style letter:

- Return address block (sender's information), date, and signature block are indented to the halfway point or just beyond.

MODIFIED BLOCK FORMAT SAMPLE

100 Anywhere Street *(sender's street address)*
Atlanta, GA 30301 *(sender's city, state & zip code)*
May 1, 20__ *(current date) (4X)*

Mrs. Maria Lopez, President *(recipient's name & title, if applicable)*
ABC Incorporated *(company name)*
1612 Industrial Avenue *(recipient's street address)*
Pittsburgh, PA 15227 *(recipient's city, state & zip code) (2X)*

Dear Mrs. Lopez: *(greeting/salutation, followed with a colon) (2X)*

As the recipient of this year's *Make a Difference* scholarship, I would like to thank you and the entire scholarship committee for bestowing this honor upon me. I will continue to work hard to make a difference as I enter my college years. *(2X)*

I plan to use this scholarship money to pay for books and tuition this coming year. I look forward to getting involved in college organizations and may be rushing a sorority. As they say, "the world is my oyster!"

For your use and enjoyment, I am enclosing a picture from the Chamber of Commerce meeting when I received the scholarship check. If I can be of any assistance to your organization in the future, do not hesitate to contact me at beth@gmail.com. I would enjoy being an ambassador for ABC at any time.

Respectfully, *(4-5X)*

Beth Carey
(signature in blue or black ink on hard copies only)

Beth Carey *(typed name of sender)*
Trimont HS Valedictorian *(2X) (typed sender title)*

Enc. *(warning of additional enclosed document)*
cc: Mechelle Morris, VP *(individuals who will get a copy of this letter)*
Linda Sue Latchman, Marketing Director

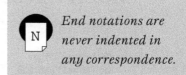

The modified semi-block letter format is the final layout format I will discuss. It has been around the longest and requires a little more knowledge to use as the spacing design includes multiple indentations to be correct.

End notations are never indented in any correspondence.

A sample *MODIFIED SEMI-BLOCK* LETTER layout appears on the next page and illustrates the use of letterhead. Letterhead paper can be pre-printed and inserted into a printer or copier making it a favorite to use. Letterhead can also be in a saved electronic version, accessed easily from a saved file on the computer. Either way, I would again like to point out that the date is the first piece of written information when letterhead is used.

Here are the unique components for a modified semi-block letter:

- The return address block (sender's information), date, and signature block are indented to the halfway point or just beyond.
- Each paragraph is indented five spaces (consider using the tab key or styles to ensure all indents start at the same point in the body of the letter).

MODIFIED SEMI-BLOCK FORMAT SAMPLE

Beth Carey, Author
Trail Ahead Publishing
100 Anywhere Street
Atlanta, GA 30301

L.I.F.E.

404-555-5555   LEARNING INFORMATION FOR EVERYDAY
beth@learninginfoforeveryday.com

May 1, 20__ *(Current date) (4X)*

Mrs. Anna Yoder, Principal *(recipient's name & title)*
Bethel Middle School *(company name)*
1000 Library Road *(recipient's street address)*
Pittsburgh, PA 15102 *(recipient's city, state & zip code) (2X)*

Dear Mrs. Yoder: *(greeting/salutation, followed with a colon) (2X)*

  As the author of *L.I.F.E. (Learning Information For Everyday) Book 1 - Basic Knowledge* and Book 2 - *Social Skills,* I am writing to let you know there are only a few days left in the school year in which I am available to do a workshop for your parents *(or faculty),* so please book now!

  I have included some additional information with this letter and encourage you to visit <u>www.learninginfoforeveryday.com</u>. I am available to present evenings or days and want you to know that I carefully picked your school as a community that would truly benefit from this workshop.

  I will look forward to hearing from you soon.

       Yours Truly, *(4-5X)*

       Beth Carey
       (signature in ink, on hard copies only)
       Beth Carey *(typed name of sender)*
       Author *(2X) (typed title of sender)*

Enclosures (2)

The modified block and semi-modified block style lend themselves to giving a message some additional flare or panache although they are a more "old school" approach. A writer can make the decision as to which style suits them best for each correspondence. The most important thing for teenagers to take away from this letter writing section is that there are many resources to consult when learning to write a professional looking letter. Use these resources to guarantee set-up is done correctly and to make the best impression.

16. List the names of all fifty states in the U.S. with the corresponding two-letter abbreviation for each state. (No using a resource other than your brain!)

State	Abbreviation	State	Abbreviation	State	Abbreviation
Alabama	AL	Louisiana	LA	Ohio	OH
Alaska	AK	Maine	ME	Oklahoma	OK
Arizona	AZ	Maryland	MD	Oregon	OR
Arkansas	AR	Massachusetts	MA	Pennsylvania	PA
California	CA	Michigan	MI	Rhode Island	RI
Colorado	CO	Minnesota	MN	South Carolina	SC
Connecticut	CT	Mississippi	MS	South Dakota	SD
Delaware	DE	Missouri	MO	Tennessee	TN
Florida	FL	Montana	MT	Texas	TX
Georgia	GA	Nebraska	NE	Utah	UT
Hawaii	HI	Nevada	NV	Vermont	VT
Idaho	ID	New Hampshire	NH	Virginia	VA
Illinois	IL	New Jersey	NJ	Washington	WA
Indiana	IN	New Mexico	NM	West Virginia	WV
Iowa	IA	New York	NY	Wisconsin	WI
Kansas	KS	North Carolina	NC	Wyoming	WY
Kentucky	KY	North Dakota	ND		

Funny how hard it can be to name all 50 states even though we all learned them in elementary school. And when it comes to the abbreviations, adults (depending on current age) can be at a real disadvantage assisting teens because state abbreviations have changed since many adults were kids. Historically, state abbreviations started with a capital letter and were followed by a range of lower case letters and a period (e.g., Florida was Fla., New Hampshire was N. Hamp.). Some states required the use of two capitals with a period after each letter (e.g., New York was N.Y., Rhode Island was R.I.), but not anymore!

Teens actually have it easier today as they were taught the state abbreviations with two capital letters and no punctuation. However, many still struggle when the state name is not written out in full. I want young people to know that using the correct abbreviation is especially important when writing letters and addressing an envelope. Correct use of state abbreviations is needed to avoid mail delays as well as to show proper awareness of new standards.

 17. Address an envelope to your best friend's parent(s). Must include appropriate spacing, a return address, two letter state abbreviations, and a drawn on stamp in the proper location.

 The layout for proper envelope addressing is below:

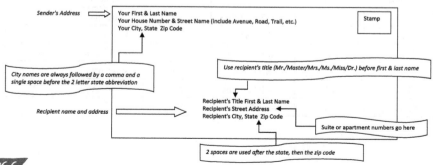

Sender's Address ⟹ Your First & Last Name
Your House Number & Street Name (Include Avenue, Road, Trail, etc.)
Your City, State Zip Code

Stamp

Use recipient's title (Mr./Master/Mrs./Ms./Miss/Dr.) before first & last name

City names are always followed by a comma and a single space before the 2 letter state abbreviation

Recipient name and address ⟹ Recipient's Title First & Last Name
Recipient's Street Address
Recipient's City, State Zip Code

Suite or apartment numbers go here

2 spaces are used after the state, then the zip code

Currently, the USPS (United States Postal Service) requests addresses on envelopes and packages to be typed or printed clearly with a pen or permanent marker so the address is legible from an arm's length away without the use of commas or periods. (Preferably in all capital letters.) However, I am suggesting that teens learn how to use the commas and periods on envelopes (because they will be delivered either way) to reduce confusion and errors between letter writing rules and envelope addressing guidelines. The choice is ultimately up to the writer!

Here is a sample utilizing actual names and illustrating the USPS recommendation for clarity:

The US Postal Service will periodically change the price of postage, therefore increasing the cost of a letter stamp. Today, USPS offers "Forever Stamps" that can be used indefinitely, even if the price of a stamp increases after purchase.

JOE SMOE
101 MAIN STREET
ATLANTA GA 30301

Stamp

MR & MRS TODD JENKINS
1600 ELM STREET APT 12B
DANVILLE PA 17821

"Mrs. Carey, where does the stamp go on an envelope?"

"Josiah, do you really not know that? And why are you asking me?"

"Well, we have to write thank you notes to our senior project facilitator for English class and I'm not sure. We have to turn in an addressed envelope with a stamp. I don't want Mrs. Bentley to know I don't know, so I thought I'd ask you." Josiah said with a smirk.

There are times when a person needs to send correspondence to a specific individual, through another person or a company name. This intermediary is then responsible for transferring the mail piece to the intended addressee. Teenagers usually don't think of this scenario, but they need to know what to do in this case. When sending a letter to a person who doesn't typically work or live at a particular address, addressing the envelope includes c/o (In Care Of). The c/o is placed under the recipient's name, just before the name of the company or person who regularly resides there. It would look like this:

If a letter is intended for a particular person who can be permanently found at an address, but may not be the same as the legal addressee (i.e., a company name), use Attn: or ATTN standing for "Attention" before the person's name. It would look like this on an envelope:

18. "Memo" is derived from what Latin word?

🔑 Memorandum

19. When and where would you find a memo being used?

🔑 In businesses for interoffice communication-can be used anytime one employee wants to communicate with another-can be used by anyone for short and concise correspondence

For the most part, emails have taken the place of a hard copy memorandum in the work place and in personal situations. However, paper memos are still used and the memo format is used even when sending electronically, so teenagers need to be familiar with it. If you think about it, an email header looks much like a memo heading, so teenagers will grasp this written correspondence with little trouble.

The purpose of a memo is to inform, bring attention to something, and solve problems with the interests of their reader at the forefront. They can be a formal or an informal form of correspondence and vary in length although typically they are less than one page. Memos are easy to use with no addresses, greeting/salutation, or closing and are usually done on company letterhead. The word Memo or Memorandum is placed at the top the page.

20. List the required headings used on a memorandum.

🔑 To, From, Date, Subject (or Re for Regarding)-Company Name would be the first heading on the rare occasion letterhead is not used

Each heading title is followed with a colon for punctuation. Typically the headings are left justified, but it is a personal preference (or company precedence) that may cause a writer to deviate and space the headings by lining up the colons. Teens also should know that they are free to capitalize all the letters in a heading or just capitalize the first letter of each heading (i.e., To: or TO:).

 21. Write a memo announcing to the family that you have just won a trip to Disneyland and they are all invited to go. Must be in correct memo format and include all headings with proper punctuation.

 Memo content will vary, but the layout needs to look like the memo on the next page.

 Here are the steps for constructing a memo:

→ Label the document by placing the word Memo or Memorandum at the top of the page (below the letterhead if one is used).
→ Double space the four headings.
→ After the "To:" heading, place recipient's name and title—for multiple people, use a list format and place beneath each other.
→ After the "From:" heading, place your name and title (if applicable).
→ After the "Date:" heading, state the current date (including the year).
→ After the "Subject:" heading, create a concise phrase summarizing topic to be covered within.
→ Single space content with a blank line between paragraphs.
→ Use no indentions.
→ Keep message content brief with an introduction and summary.

MEMO

TO: Tom Carey, Father
           Ben Carey, Son
           Leah Carey, Daughter

FROM: Beth Carey, Mother

DATE: May 1, 20__

RE: Trip to Disneyland

I have a huge announcement that will excite and please everyone … we are all going to Disneyland this summer!!

If you remember, I bought a raffle ticket from the local high school baseball team at the grocery store last month. The drawing to win the trip was last Friday and my name was picked, so we have an all expense trip for five nights and six days to Disneyland in Anaheim, CA.

We leave August 1st and return the 6th. Our hotel is called Park Fun Hotel and is within walking distance of Disney. Mark your calendars!!

Re: stands for Regarding and can be used in place of Subject as a heading.

Here is a generic illustration of a memo:

MEMORANDUM

To: *(readers' names and job titles (if applicable), with a comma in between)*

From: *(writer's name and job title (if applicable), with a comma in between)*

Date: *(complete current date)*

Subject: *(what the memo is about, specific in nature)*

Content will start here with an introduction and continue in paragraph form. Explain why you are writing the memo and the action to be taken. End with a brief conclusion and always be concise.

<u>Misc. Vocab</u> - Define the following computer related words...

22. Downloading

 Taking a file (program, document, spreadsheet, etc.) and transferring to a computer from a non-local source attached to a computer (basically, the internet)–receiving data to a local system from a remote system

23. Installing

⑨ Putting a program onto a computer, enabling it to work, so it can be utilized

24. Copying

⑨ Duplicating a file by taking it from one local source/ place to another local source (e.g., taking a file stored on an external jump drive and duplicating it onto a computer hard drive)

25. Sexting

⑨ Remarks and/or pictures of a sexual nature on a cell phone

All teenagers must avoid sexting and transmitting any form of inappropriate language or photos over an electronic device. Daily there are news reports about the harmful outcomes of such behavior — ranging from hurt feelings to suicide. This is against the law if under 18 years old and it is damaging reputations, causing embarrassment, and destroying self-esteem. A discussion worth having among teenagers.

26. What is your email address? Is it appropriate to use throughout adulthood?

⑨ Answers will vary

The answer here only matters if the address given is socially unacceptable in terms of having negative connotations and a teen is in denial about what is "appropriate." Emails, such as *partygirl247@, bigboytoy@, daddysgirl@, someguywithemu@,* or *gamerguru1@,* give the wrong message to others. To illustrate this point, I will say that as much as we all love a party girl, an employer would hesitate to offer a job to one and college admission counselors would also be reluctant to offer a scholarship to one.

In an email address, sexual innuendos are never OK — period. Youthful addresses need to be replaced with simple, easy to recall addresses that are serious in nature. Everyone needs to watch out for unintended words that arise from combining abbreviations as these too may create a new word with unfavorable consequences.

I suggest using your given name. A combination of a person's first and last name (with or without a period or underscore in between), use of the first initial and last name, or the last name with initials to follow all work well. Teens are important and should express that through a professional sounding email address. There is also a benefit in this type of "personal marketing or branding." If an email address relates to a name, another person (employer or otherwise) doesn't have to work as hard to associate it with an individual. If an email isn't related to your name, it's easily forgotten (and we never want to be forgotten or overlooked).

27. List 5 rules of social decorum related to being online (i.e., netiquette).

   ⑨ Here are some ideas, but allow for any reasonable ideas given:

- Don't say or post anything you would not want printed on the front page of the newspaper or your grandmother to see

"Mom, check this out!" Bee exclaimed as she set her computer down in front of her mom.

"Oh my. Is that your cousin playing beer pong? And that doesn't look like a Marlboro to me!" Lisa said as she pointed to the picture.

"Yep. And look at what the post says. I didn't even know a person could put that many nasty words in one sentence," Bee said with a giggle.

"Should I call my sister about this?"

"No. I hate to do it, but I'm just going to block him, even though he is my cousin. He posts stuff like this all the time and I can't have this on my Facebook feed."

"I'm sorry honey, but I think you are being smart. Next time you are together you should mention to him that he needs to think before posting stuff like that."

- Begin email messages with a greeting
- Identify yourself in header or at the end of an email message
- Include a subject line in emails
- Avoid using subject line "as" your email
- Avoid personal, serious, and emotional topics (i.e., breaking up with someone, resigning from a job, delivering bad news, etc.)
- Be brief
- Avoid gossip and foul language
- Use as a way to find and keep friends/family- not as a vehicle to "creep" on others

It was a peaceful September evening when I noticed a Facebook message. Much to my surprise, it was an ex-student named Miranda. She was reaching out to thank me for everything I taught her in high school. She was about to graduate college with a degree in marketing and a certificate in advertising and sales (the subjects I taught). She went on to share how I influenced her career decision and helped create memorable times and learning experiences. We scheduled a lunch and have stayed connected on Facebook ever since. Now that's good use of social media!

- Acknowledge and return messages promptly
- Don't copy everyone you know on a message (respect people's inbox)
- Don't participate in the spread of spam or junk mail
- Use appropriate emoticons (emotion icons) and do not overuse them
- Proofread for spelling, grammar, sentence structure, and intent of message
  - Watch the use of all caps as it portrays anger and/or yelling
  - Avoid abbreviations when writing emails
  - Avoid sarcasm as it is often misinterpreted
  - Never be hateful or disgusting in words or pictures
  - Don't use it as your personal brag book or complaint center
  - Back-up data regularly so you don't inconvenience others when you lose data
  - Switch it up once in awhile and use face-to-face interaction

 In work situations, you may or may not need to "copy all" on correspondence.

Auto correct can come back to haunt you, so proofread every time!

Jessie had just graduated from nursing school and was looking for a job. She also was thrilled to be pregnant with her first child and was posting a baby update weekly. Everything seemed to be "coming up roses" as far as she was concerned.

Tuesday, she interviewed with a doctor in her town and really felt good upon leaving the office, but a week went by and she didn't get a call or email with a job offer. One day she ran into the receptionist who worked with the doctor in the grocery store. After exchanging the normal pleasantries, Jessie came right out and inquired why she hadn't gotten a job offer. The receptionist glanced at her shoes and quietly said, "Well, the doctor saw that you were pregnant on your Facebook page and decided to not hire someone who would need maternity leave soon. Don't get me wrong, he liked you, but is claiming a more qualified applicant was offered the job. I'm sorry."

Potential bosses look at Facebook and web pages of prospective employees. Even if you are not the person making crude and rude comments, it can be held against you for having associates who do.

What to share on Facebook is a personal choice, but think first.

Netiquette is the term given to etiquette to be used while communicating on the internet. It can be applied to web surfing, email, and all social media (texting will be addressed in the next question). And although the following concepts aren't truly etiquette, they may have been given as an answer to the question and are worthwhile points to mention:

1. Be wary when online as not everything is true on electronic airways and dangers do lurk.
2. Do not impersonate anyone online or use a false identity.

3. It is illegal to copy (words or pictures) without permission and one must give credit when re-tweeting, blogging, posting, etc.
4. Do not divulge personal information over the internet.

In addition to the concepts listed previously, I personally would like to drive home the use of the *24 hour rule*. This rule suggests a max of 24 hours to acknowledge and return any correspondence online (especially work related emails). This practice is an admirable goal that decreases procrastination and reduces stress (two things many of us suffer from).

I also want to take a minute and address the parents and adult readers, *on behalf of teens*, by asking you to reflect on your social media behaviors. Because we are asking teenagers to adhere to certain online protocol, adults too have some rules to follow. To avoid embarrassing a teen or driving a wedge into your relationship, strive to adhere to these guidelines related to social media:

1. Refrain from commenting on posts and/or tweets without checking to see what level of participation a teen is comfortable with for you (related to their friends and their own posts/tweets).
2. Do not post pictures of a teen without getting their OK.
3. Have a discussion with a given teen *before* making a friend or follow request to one of their acquaintances. Perhaps mention in person you would like to follow or be someone's friend and wait for that adolescent to reach out to you.
4. Be a good social media role model — monitor what you write.
5. Have an open dialogue with teens about their use of social media.

28. List 5 rules of social decorum related to "texting"
(i.e., textiquette).

Answers will vary, but allow for any reasonable
ideas given:
- Not to be done in the presence of
others-excuse yourself and make it quick
- Alert recipients that you are going to end a
message string
- Limit abbreviations
- Be aware of time zones
- Put names with phone numbers to easily
ensure message is going to correct person
- Not to be used for sending invitations to
formal events
- Use vibrate feature instead of an
audible alert
- Avoid when doing anything that requires
attentiveness (i.e., driving, walking, eating)
- Do not use for bad or sad news
- Avoid during a meeting or conference (give the
facilitator or speaker your undivided attention)
- Avoid inappropriate profile pictures as
social media can be linked to cell phone
address books
- Avoid sending messages containing anything
that you are not willing to say face to face
- Avoid sarcasm as it is easily misconstrued
- No bullying, threatening, mean, or
sexual messages

Many teens apply real care with cell phone use and I applaud them for that because it isn't always the easiest thing to do. I encourage teens to step away from their cell phone for periods of time and would like more adults to role model this behavior (a small fantasy of mine, I must confess). In my experience, people resist the idea at first, but when they will see the freedom and joy it brings, they start to appreciate the concept and are very honest about their potential "unhealthy attachment" to the device (which creates some good laughs at times).

Additionally, I hope teens are aware of the stories regularly in the news about unexpected stranger rage tied to cell phone misuse. Reports include deaths due to texting and driving, health issues as a result of excessive cell phone usage, and cyber-bullying which continues to be on the rise. My main concern about overuse of smart phones is whether their use could be leading to weaker people skills in *both the real* and *digital realm of life*. I don't want adolescents missing experiences and sights because their eyes are looking down at a phone screen. Can we strive for some middle ground here? Experience is the most valuable LIFE skill and it requires an on-going series of interaction and activities between humans — a concept that has not changed and will not change through the decades.

///////////////////////////

Written correspondence — communication that lasts forever! Something all teens can to take to heart and start adapting their habits now. It is an excellent way to put your best foot forward by showing maturity, English skills, and proper etiquette. I tell teens all the time, "A person knows they are ready for adulthood when they can use electronic devices as a tool rather than a lifeline, they can create a business format letter, and they use their personalized stationery on a regular basis!" (LOL)

Young people will not gravitate to corresponding using pen and paper, so LET IT GO! Ease, time factors, and generational habits will have them reaching for a phone or computer nine times out of ten. However, applying writing with appropriate etiquette and format electronically will go a long way and when a teen does send a handwritten note, it will have major significance.

⑨ Wrap-Up

As I stated in the introduction, teenagers learning and practicing proper social skills is a passion for me. I want young people to understand the implications of *not* utilizing proper knowledge and skills related to general etiquette, personal guidelines, dining protocol, oral communication, and written correspondence and start improving today. My wish is that they *never* have a negative consequence in their lifetime for not knowing and utilizing the concepts in this book.

I hope the **adult readers** strive to assist any and all teenagers, not just those who share their bloodline. I expect **teen readers** to rise above the bad habits of their peers and proudly exhibit the right actions learned within this book and become good role models for future generations.

L.I.F.E. — Independence (Book 3 in the series) will be filled with questions related to transitioning from high school to the next phase by preparing for a job/career, understanding the basics of finance/money management, and being ready for independent traveling. And if you haven't taken advantage of the topics in Book 1 ***(L.I.F.E. — Basic Knowledge)***, it is never too late to get a copy and start checking for comprehension on topics related to home life skills, community, government, and study habits.

As always, I hope you enjoyed your journey through this book *and* will benefit from the growth that takes place anytime an adult and a young person engage in conversation and activities!

More Information Available

learninginfoforeveryday.com
facebook.com/learninginfoforeveryday
twitter.com/beth_life_
pinterest.com/lifelearninginf/

L.I.F.E. is available in print and eBook versions through Amazon. Additional outlets may include: Barnes & Noble, Books-A-Million, and select brick and mortar bookstores.

If your group is interested in a personal appearance or speaking engagement, contact me at beth@learninginfoforeveryday.com

Acknowledgements

I would like to thank my family and friends for the continued support ...
> *you are the foundation for all that is good in life.*

To Jason, Mary Helen, Sue, Elspeth, Sue Mac, Margie, Tom, and Kerith ...
> *your editing and insight has been phenomenal.*

To Augi ...
> *your artistic talents are admired.*

To Kimberly and the Jera staff ...
> *your patience and unending assistance has been the backbone of this project.*

And to all the adults and teenagers who are engaging because of the L.I.F.E. series ...
> *may you continue the challenge and be successful in your life journey.*

About The Author

Beth Carey is a retired teacher from the Atlanta, Georgia, area with a passion for aiding teenagers as they prepare for life. Her mission in and out of the classroom has always been to help teens with their journey into the real world so they become happy, responsible, independent adults.

She received an undergraduate degree in marketing education from Indiana University of Pennsylvania and master's degree from Georgia State University in vocational leadership. She taught high school in various states during her 30 year tenure and was awarded Georgia Marketing Teacher of the Year in 2006 and voted by her peers to receive Teacher of the Year at her home high school in 2011. Her students earned multiple awards on the regional, state, and international level of competition through their involvement in the Association of Marketing Students (DECA), under her leadership. Her ability to use a dose of daily humor and love while setting high expectations and limits in the classroom allowed teens to thrive. Her focus was giving teenagers understanding and real life problem-solving skills related to the world of business.

When not with adolescents, Beth loves to cook, travel, and spend time with her husband and children at the lake. She invites you to "Challenge" Teen's Basic Knowledge, Social Skills, and Independence Readiness. *L.I.F.E. (Learning Information For Everyday)* is a book series targeting those who share her goals.

Beth would love to hear your thoughts, stories and suggestions, so feel free to contact her at www.learninginfoforeveryday.com or beth@learninginfoforeveryday.com.